FRONT LINE OBSERVER

A CASUALTY REPORT FROM THE BATTLE FOR THE FAMILY

BY

MARK LOFTIN

Bloomington, IN 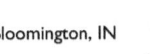  Milton Keynes, UK

authorHOUSE®

AuthorHouse™
1663 Liberty Drive, Suite 200
Bloomington, IN 47403
www.authorhouse.com
Phone: 1-800-839-8640

AuthorHouse™ UK Ltd.
500 Avebury Boulevard
Central Milton Keynes, MK9 2BE
www.authorhouse.co.uk
Phone: 08001974150

First published by AuthorHouse   3/21/2007

ISBN: 978-1-4259-9455-6 (sc)

Library of Congress Control Number: 2007901364

Printed in the United States of America
Bloomington, Indiana

This book is printed on acid-free paper.

To Debbie

For serving on the front line alongside me
For helping me remember
For proofreading
For your time
For believing in me
For marrying me and sticking with me.

TABLE OF CONTENTS

INTRODUCTION

This is not about me. It is not my story or my memoirs, but observations that we have made while serving on the front line of the battle for our culture, our families, and our kids. These observations that my wife, Debbie, and I have made come from three sources. A few come from court or other referral records that come with the kids who have lived with us. Some come from what the kids and their families have told us about their lives and choices. The great majority come from what we have actually seen, heard, and experienced first hand in our work with kids and families. I have been careful to include only what we have actually observed during our experience as house parents, children's home directors, and volunteers. These are not what we have heard from others in our profession, or what we have been taught in school or training, or what we believe, feel, wish, or think, but actual observations. I will not tell any stories, quote any kids or parents, or bring up any issues that have not been directly observed in our work.

This is not scientific research, or my dissertation for a doctorate, but I feel like if you have chosen to read this, you deserve to know how we are qualified to make these observations. I will try to tell you just enough about us to describe our experience, and how we are qualified to make these observations. I will try not to talk so much about us that it bores you. In some way or another, we have been working with kids since we were college kids ourselves. It was in 1977, when I was not yet 20, that I began to attend Moody Bible Institute in Chicago, after two years at Oklahoma State University. One of the requirements at MBI was to be involved in some practical work experience there in Chicago that would relate to and enhance our education. I was assigned to Crusader Youth Outreach, which was a ministry that worked with kids and teenagers in an area of Chicago northwest of downtown. The work included kids clubs, sports, camping, and other relationship-building outings. The first time I met with the other volunteer staff of CYO, I met Debbie Powell, who had already been volunteering for a couple of years, and who is the finest lady I have ever known. We spent lots of time working together there until I finished my degree in 1981, and in that time our relationship progressed from friends to a couple with a growing love, who wanted to spend the rest of their lives together. We were married on December 29, 1979.

Both of us wanted to keep working with teenagers, in ways that build relationships and give them chances to grow into adults who make good decisions. We wanted to give kids who needed to change the direction of their lives a safe, healthy, nurturing home where we could teach and encourage them. Many of the kids we knew in Chicago seemed stuck in a destructive cycle of bad choices that repeated the mistakes of their parents or other kids around them. Some wanted to get out of the cycle, but staying in the same neighborhood with the same peers made this almost impossible, without help. Being house parents would give us the chance to work closely together and with the kind of kids to whom we felt called, and in an atmosphere that could encourage healthy growth into adults who could make good choices and maybe break the cycle.

As soon as I graduated, we spent the summer working at Camp Hickory, north of Chicago, which was a good transition into our goal of being house parents. In the fall, we began working with New Horizons Youth Ministries. This is a great organization, with locations in the USA, Canada, and the Dominican Republic, which works with teenagers who are low achievers but have high potential. We trained for three months in the group home in Marion, Indiana, and then spent all of 1982 and 1983 at the boarding school on the Dominican Republic. We were parents in a house of eight boys, who were mostly from middle- to upper- class homes in the US Midwest, and had been sent there by their parents. This program emphasized living up to your potential by building character strength and developing a mature, positive attitude. The location out of the country took them away from negative influences, from peers to television, and was a great chance for them to start over. Meanwhile, US based NHYM staff worked with the families.

Our next house parent position was with Cedar Ridge Children's Home in Williamsport, Maryland. We had a house of twelve boys, ages ten to fourteen, who were mostly from the Baltimore area and were in state custody. These boys came from abusive situations and dysfunctional families, and had emotional and behavior problems. Many of them lived there with us a long time, and moved to the house next door to us when they were older. These two house parent positions prepared us to take the next step: directing a residential program ourselves.

Between October of 1987 and June, 2006 Debbie and I were directors of the New Life Youth Home program, which was a ministry of the Dyersburg-Dyer County Union Mission, in Tennessee. This was a live-in position, and gave us the chance to run our own small home, where before we had been one of a number of house parent couples in a larger residential organization. Ours was the only house, and the home was much more like a large foster family than an institution. Almost all of the kids who lived there with us had been in state custody. They may have been abused, abandoned, or neglected, may have been unruly, may have committed delinquent acts, or any combination of these. Our main responsibility was to concentrate on helping these kids to grow to the point to where they were ready to return to their family, move to an adoptive family, or to be on their own. We provided structure, stability, supervision, and safety, and we tried to be good examples. Our hope was that while they were there they would develop some maturity, skills, and character strengths so that they could recognize the causes of their being away from their family, how to prevent this from happening again, and break out of the cycle. We want them to bring their kids to visit us, but we don't want their kids to live with us. For seven years we had just girls at New Life Youth Home, and for the rest of the time we had both boys and girls. The great majority of kids had been between the ages of 12 and 19, and they were with us anywhere from one night to over six years. There were up to 11 kids living there with us at a time. Relationships are the key; these were and are our kids, not our clients. There have been more than 200 kids who stayed with us at NLYH, and nearly 300 in total since we started doing residential work. Most of the observations in this book come from our time at NLYH, because we had been there so long, and because there was much more family and other background information available to us about the kids than there had been at the other group homes.

I began this book while working at NLYH in the fall of 2005. Except for the last chapter, I finished my book in the spring of 2006, just before I began my next adventure working with kids. Debbie and I are still in Dyersburg, and still with the Mission. The after-school clubs for kids at the Mission Youth Center and the summer day camp are where I'm serving now. Debbie helps with the high school club and with families who come to the Mission for help.

Privacy rules and good manners prevent me from using the full names of our kids. At times I will use a first name, and other times I will use initials or not use a name at all. I will not use the parents' names.

I could have written an entire book of funny or sad stories, or funny or sad things our kids have said. I could have written a book that only pointed out the observations that we have made of why kids end up living with us or what is damaging our kids and our society. Instead, I put all kinds of observations together, because our lives with the kids have been like that; not one or the other, but layered together in the same child or family at the same time. Our work has been both a source of joy and frustration, so both emotions are in this book. I have decided to share with you the pleasure and hope of our work, but also I have a responsibility to share the observations of problems we see that scare us for the future and beg for a cure. One single overriding issue will be presented to you-which will be the trait that is by far the most common denominator with all of our kids-along with proposals to work for a solution. Like a scientist who finds the cause and a cure for a deadly disease, we feel responsible to share what we have observed, along with ideas for a cure. When I started making notes of my observations to share in a book, I didn't approach my work with an agenda to make a point. However, while I was writing my observations, the issue of what is the root cause of kids being placed in foster care stared me in the face until I couldn't ignore it.

Life is complicated, especially with a home full of teenagers, and since our experiences include events that stir all of the following emotions and elicit all of these reactions, I will mix:

happy and sad;

funny and depressing;

wise and stupid;

perverted and pure;

silly and meaningful;

ridiculous and common sense;

satisfying and frustrating;

humorous and serious;

maddening and pleasing.

I invite you to:

get pleasure from the happy, and feel for the sad;

enjoy the funny, and listen to the depressing;

learn from the wise, and marvel at the stupid;

recognize the perverted, and strive for the pure;

laugh at the silly, and contemplate the meaningful;

expose the ridiculous, and appreciate the common sense;

celebrate the satisfying, and solve the frustrating;

smile at the humorous, and learn from the serious;

see what you can do about the maddening, and get pleasure from the pleasing; and relate to all of them.

Making up stories, exaggerating, or embellishing is not necessary; these are as we have seen or heard or are in the record. Some observations are here just because they happened or for the entertainment value. Others point out problems in the morals of our society, and the destructive consequences to children and families that a lack of good, strong morals has caused. Some observations are just to tell the story, and others beg us for solutions or preventions for the destruction of families. What gives pleasure is meant to be shared. What damages or destroys our children and families also damages or destroys our society, culture, and nation, and needs to be exposed.

Chapter 1

STORY TIME

Christy made some muffins for the middle school 4H contest. They were pretty good, so in the morning she put them on a paper plate, covered them with plastic wrap, and put the plate on the seat next to her in our van. Of course, on the way to school they fell off the seat and rolled around on the rubber floor of the van, ending up on the inside step by the side doors coated in hair, dirt, and I wouldn't want to guess what else. She screamed, "I'm taking them anyway!" as the kids chased the muffins around the van. She gathered them up, wiped them off, and headed to the unsuspecting judges. She came out of school that afternoon, bragging that the teachers had liked them and awarded her second prize in the school! I wonder what the third place muffins tasted like. We never told the teachers, until now.

Mike caught a snake in the pasture, and wanted to keep it for a pet. I didn't recognize it, and we couldn't find one like it in any of our books. I told the boys that we would not be keeping it unless I could be sure that it wasn't poisonous. I thought the subject was over until Mike came to me the next day. He said that he knew the snake wasn't poisonous, so I asked him how he could be sure. The answer was, "Yesterday I let the snake bite me in the face twice, and I'm still OK!" He even had other boys as witnesses, and showed me the tiny bite marks. We made a new rule that day. I wonder if Mike is still alive, or if he ever found a poisonous snake.

George like turtles better than snakes. In the pond near our house there were snapping turtles as big as basketballs that would bury themselves in the mud in the shallow water. They had killed some of the ducks, and one time a turtle had such a grip on a tree limb that we were able to pick it up by the limb, until the turtle bit all the way through it until it broke. George came running up to me one day, holding a huge, angry turtle by the tail, and told me he had figured out how to catch turtles. "I just look for bubbles coming up through the mud and then reach down in the mud with my hands and grab 'em!" After my jaw dropped and my eyes bugged out for a second, I asked, "What would have happened if you grabbed his face?!" He just shrugged, "I dunno." We made another new rule that day.

One of our girls, who had gotten pregnant a couple of years after she went home, told us, "I don't even like the boy and he isn't my boyfriend." When we asked her why she had sex with him then, she said, "This girl had sex with my boyfriend so I had sex with her boyfriend to get revenge on her!" In this family, the cycle will continue because there is another child who, like her mom, will grow up without a dad.

This same girl had another baby who was accidentally shot to death at home by a young cousin who had been playing with a loaded gun. This child had access to the gun because the family didn't value the safety of the children enough to keep loaded guns safely locked away.

Debbie was too sick to cook, and our eight boys at Escuela Caribe in the Dominican Republic would need supper. Eric volunteered to cook while I did yard work with the rest of the boys. He knew how to make pancakes, following a recipe that claimed to feed thirty people, which Debbie often used to feed the ten of us. Convenience foods were not available where we lived, outside of Jarabacoa, so everything was made from scratch. A few minutes into the job, Eric came outside to tell me he had accidentally doubled the baking powder, and to ask me what he should do. I told him to double everything else, and we would just have pancakes tomorrow, too. When I came in from chores, the kitchen looked like an "I Love Lucy" episode. Eric was a mess, and every serving bowl and pot we had was full of pancake batter. Eric explained that when he was doubling the other ingredients, he put too much of something in, so he doubled everything else again. Then, while he was doing that, he again put in too much of something, so he had to double everything else again. Pancake batter to the fourth power! It amazed me that after all that, he got the ratio of ingredients just right for perfect pancakes.

The pancakes were great! Well, at least the first day they were. The second day they were pretty good; the third day they were OK, and the fourth day I actually ate a few. Our budget was too tight to waste food, and there was little freezer space. I imagine Eric is using his math and logic skills somewhere, but I hope it isn't in a nuclear lab.

A girl's mom told her on the phone that she (the mom) had a new boyfriend, who wanted to take both of them to California. Mom told her to cut class and meet her at a certain place in town, so the girl obediently did it, but mom and the boyfriend never showed up. It got late, and now our girl is scared; she knows that she is a runaway from her home and will also be in trouble for skipping class. She finally called an aunt, and ended up safely back home with us. Her mom had just changed her mind.

Some of our kids keep in touch when they are adults. One of our girls called to tell us that she had found a phone number in her husband's pants while she was doing laundry. She called the number and it turned out to be another of our girls! When confronted, her husband said the other girl had given him the phone number, and he was just holding on to it for his cousin. They are still together, but now another girl (not one of ours, at least yet) claims her baby is his.

C told a teacher that she couldn't get her homework done because we made her dance at a strip club every night. She also bragged that we had taken all of our girls (some of them black) to a KKK rally in Memphis, and her grandpa was there with the KKK. I have a deal with some of the teachers: I won't believe anything crazy about them if they don't believe anything crazy the kids say about us, until we check with each other.

J came to us as a thirteen-year old who claimed she was pregnant. (She wasn't.) She claimed to be pregnant or to already have a baby her entire four years here. (She didn't.) She even took photos of other women's babies to school and told people it was her baby. There was some drama when people recognized one of the babies she claimed to be hers. She was seventeen when she spent a weekend home, and got pregnant by a cousin of her sister's boyfriend. When her pregnancy test was positive the next month she said, "See? I told you so!" Probably the longest pregnancy on record. By the way, he returned to Mexico when he found out about the baby.

Danny was with us in a sporting goods store in the mall in Jackson, TN. There was a free- standing display in the middle of the store of an outdoor basketball goal, surrounded by a stack of balls for sale. Danny assumed the pole was bolted to the floor. It wasn't. He called out the famous words, "Hey, y'all, watch this!" and ran up with a ball to do a slam dunk. (Did I mention he was the school heavyweight wrestler?) As he hung on the rim, the entire backboard, pole, and display came crashing down with him, and he was flat on his back, covered up by the backboard. (I recognized this position, from having watched him wrestle.) Customers and balls scattered. Employees scrambled to help him out from under the backboard. I didn't. There are times when I am really glad to be able to say honestly that genetically, I have nothing to do with these kids.

Some of our boys from Baltimore were disappointed that they couldn't be home to celebrate Martin Luther King's birthday. When I asked how it was celebrated, they bragged excitedly about running through their neighborhood with their friends, smashing out windows in cars and buildings. When I asked what King did and how this honors his work, all they could tell me was that he was a black man who was killed by a white man. They were surprised when I explained to them what he had done, why he had died, and how he would probably feel about smashing windows.

M was ready to spend a weekend with her mom. She hadn't been home in weeks and it was all arranged. When mom was late, she took her suitcase out on the front porch to wait. Mom never showed up or called. The next week we found out that mom had gotten drunk, got into a fight, and spent the weekend in jail. I saw a tough, aggressive girl sit on the porch and cry.

The middle school called about Charlie. It seems one of his classes was evacuated and cancelled. One of his friends had gone to a joke store, and brought a whoopee cushion and a can of "fart spray" to class. (Yes, this is what it said on the can!) He suggested that he would sit on the cushion while Charlie would use the spray. Of course, Charlie said yes. Of course, he sprayed too much. Of course the teacher didn't see the humor. When I asked why, he said, "I just wanted to know what it smelled like!" He could've just hung out in the boy's room on chili dog day. I didn't let him see me when I laughed.

A girl's mom died in a drunk driving accident while the girl lived with us. Her last communication with her mom had been a fight. She sang Amazing Grace at the funeral for her mom, but was so broken up that she couldn't finish the song. Whenever you say goodbye to your kids, make sure the last words are loving ones.

T tells us her mom has a live-in boyfriend. However, it's her dad who always comes with her mom to see her on weekends. T explained that when the boyfriend goes off for his cocaine fix on weekends, dad moves back in with mom. "Alternative lifestyles" get kids into foster care.

A boy's dad allows mom's latest boyfriend to live with them. "Alternative lifestyles" again.

DJ was walking into Wal Mart, just before Easter. There was a seven-foot-tall display of stuffed bunnies, baskets, etc. just inside the door to get your attention. What got her attention, though, were the three college- aged boys walking out the door. She turned her face to them and called out, "Hey, do you remember me? I play basketball!" Unfortunately, she had not turned her body or stopped walking. No, the display was not secured to the floor. No, I didn't help her when she screamed for help as she was trying unsuccessfully to keep the display from toppling to the floor. Yes, it was loud. Yes, I think they sure remember her, but not for her basketball skill. Yes, you can clean 'em up and dress 'em up, but you still should never take them out in public.

The middle school called, again. Would I please try to keep him from bringing his hamsters to school in his backpack? It was disrupting class. He and one of our girls each had a pet hamster, and now there were baby hamsters. The kids decided to go into the rodent business, so he was taking the momma to school to advertise and pre-sell baby hamsters. Don't you go to school to prepare yourself to make a living? Search their bags before they leave the house.

Chapter 2

OBSERVATIONS FROM THE FRONT LINE

Here are some random truths which we have learned from watching and listening to the kids who have lived with us. I will talk about some of these subjects in more detail in some of the following chapters.

Foster kids have the same traits as kids who are with their families, but are more extreme.

Kids naturally have a sense of right and wrong created in them. If you don't believe this, then try watching what happens if someone butts in front of them in the cafeteria line at school. However, this sense is undeveloped, inconsistent, hypocritical, selfish, twisted, and situational unless they have mature guidance and modeling. Kids instinctively know that there must be rules; they just want to make the rules themselves and decide when to enforce them.

Both parents following God's time-proven plan for marriage and family is the closest way to guarantee that your kids won't be removed from your family into foster care, detention, or the psychiatric ward. The opposite is also true: ignoring God's design makes casualties of your kids. This includes you, dad. The issue that is common with nearly all of the kids that we have had in foster care is not just unwed moms; its unwed, irresponsible, or disappearing dads.

Some of the other most common traits of the families of our kids have been that mom was too young to parent, abuse of drugs or alcohol, poverty, and parents who didn't complete school.

Abused or neglected kids do NOT grow up fast. There is a common but destructive myth that says such kids grow up fast. Those of us who work or live with these kids know otherwise. Experiencing something that you should never have to experience, or that should come at a more mature stage in life does not produce maturity. Having adult responsibilities forced upon you too early does not make you an adult. Instead, abused or neglected kids have teenage traits taken to the extreme as teens, or they still retain the traits of a younger child. The truth is that kids who do not have all of their needs met during each stage of their lives do not skip or grow out of those stages. Instead, these kids get emotionally stuck in these stages until these needs of each stage are met. These needs include a nurturing relationship with a mom AND a dad.

In particular, it has been made clear to us that the effect of a dad being gone, either through divorce or some other means, is usually the major factor affecting the lives of foster kids. In these situations, neither the child nor the mother have had their needs met, and a mom that does not have her needs met can't do her best job of meeting the needs of her kids. A mom who is still in the stage of trying to meet her own needs doesn't have the needs of her kids as her priority. A kid cannot grow up fast if the one responsible to nurture and set an example for him has not grown up. Don't make the mistake of seeing cockiness, disrespect or disobedience, or treating adults as peers as "grown up." The teenage girl who runs away, uses crack, or becomes a prostitute has not grown up. These are not the decisions that mature people make; they are the decisions that impulsive people make.

Abused or neglected kids do develop survival skills, but often make choices based upon immediate survival needs, without a thought for long term consequences. This is not acting "grown-up," but instead is an immature decision-making habit. Survival skills such as stealing, manipulation, hostility, or clowning can actually be signs of intelligence, but that intelligence needs to be untwisted so that it can be used to make healthy, wise choices. Toddlers know how to get what they want, but this is not a sign of being grown up. It is a sign of being smart enough to remember what works, and then to use it, again.

In the debate between genetics and environment, count me among the ones who know that the influence of genetics is undeniably strong.

Kids who are now adults, and who have lived with the biological parents for only a few months to a couple of years in their entire lifetime, will often make the same decisions that their parents made. The nut doesn't fall very far from the tree.

Most kids in foster care would rather be with their family in spite of how bad it is at home.

Countless times we have seen that girls who hate the "men" that mom chooses, and realize that it's mom's choice of those men that has contributed to their being in foster care, will still choose boys cut from the exact same mold from which their mom chose. This happens even if they swear that they will never tolerate a guy like that, or subject their daughters to an abusive situation. This also happens even if they haven't lived with their mom or haven't met their dad.

We have seen that a girl who has not had a highly involved, loving dad will often, unknowingly, choose boys or men through the eyes of her own experiences and unmet needs. Her thought processes and choices will be something like this:

> She will choose older men, someone who will meet the unmet need for a father figure. These girls will refuse to recognize that this is what they doing and why. These girls think that they're showing maturity, but they are making this choice because of an unmet childhood need.

> She thinks that a bad guy is better than no guy, and gets the same kind of guy as mom had.

> She will have poor judgment and taste in men, because she is needy, insecure, clingy, desperate, or promiscuous. She follows her mom's example, and so the cycle continues.

> She will be OK with being the "other woman," being his # 2 woman, or being used.

> She will pick men who are abusive, controlling, authoritative, and who treat her as a child.

> She will pick men who have habitually treated their previous girlfriends or wives poorly.

She will think it's normal and acceptable to be mistreated, and she doesn't deserve better.

She will think that all men are abusive, unfaithful, unable to keep commitments, or want to use her for sex. It won't matter which man she chooses, because in her life, all men are the same.

The scariest type of children we see are the psychopathic kids - the ones without a conscience. They have no thought or care for the needs or feelings of others, or for their effect on others. The second scariest type of children we see are the young, unmarried girls who are having or want to have babies.

Parents who try to be "cool" are failures - immature idiots trying to meet their own needs.

A kid's view of what God is like is often shaped by their view of what their dad is like.

People get angrier at the one who points out something wrong than the one doing wrong.

One of the differences in my generation and our kids is that these kids don't know what they want to be. They just know what they want to have, and that they want it now.

Many sports figures, too many politicians, and many more entertainment figures make bad heroes. Our kids knew that Bill Clinton was lying and that O J and Michael Jackson were guilty.

A dad can't be a real, true, hero to his kids, either, if he has abandoned them or their mom.

There are two realities: the actual reality in which we live, and perceived "reality," which is not real or true, but which is the "reality" through which kids see the world and make their choices. This perceived reality may be twisted by the media, dysfunctional families, or by abusers.

Since teenage or unwed moms and dads are bad for kids and families, then they are bad for our society, our culture, our economy, our security, our stability, and our very future.

Single moms get overwhelmed because they are without the backup, support, strength, and relief that they need. They are also often without the example or mentor that they need.

Kids will sink to whatever level we allow them to sink, like water flowing in the easiest course. We see this when kids, who've done well with us, do poorly when back with the family.

With desire and help, bad times can be used to develop good character.

Over the years, girls have become more perverted, violent, aggressive and less ladylike, but, instead of respect, safety, or equality, this behavior has gotten them less love, security, joy, confidence, pleasure, fulfillment, or true success. (Plus they're still afraid of spiders.)

When a teenager gets caught doing something, it is usually only the tip of the iceberg. Once in a while a teenager will get caught doing something wrong for the first time, because he is not very good at it. It is much more common, however, for a teenager to have done something so often that he gets overconfident and sloppy, or can't resist bragging about it.

We have learned to love unconditionally, and that this is the only real kind of love.

Enjoy each moment and each day. Celebrate progress, discovery, and growth.

Have reasonable expectations for people, including yourself. There are few quick fixes.

"That's so redneck" means the same as "That's so ghetto." When we see something like a car with a hanger for an antenna and duct tape for a window, some of our kids will say, "That's so redneck!" at the same time that others are saying "That's so ghetto!" "Ghetto" and "redneck" aren't so different, and you can really see this when kids live together.

The real skills you need for independent living are character strength, not knowledge, because someone with character strength can become wise. Our foster care contract requires us to teach independent living skills, but it's who you are, not what you know, that is most critical.

Foster kids come to expect the government or someone else to care for them indefinitely.

Trusting someone does not mean never checking on them. Accountability leads to trust.

The worst thing you can do for a manipulator, bully, or someone in denial is to allow this behavior to succeed by giving in to it. Kids will only continue to use whatever works for them.

Giving a child whatever he wants or letting him do whatever he wants and shielding him from consequences will never produce a healthy, well-adjusted, mature, appreciative child. It will produce a selfish, arrogant, demanding, disrespectful, and immature teenager.

Kids who get attention only in a crisis will learn to create a crisis; you create drama queens if your kids aren't sure of you're attention or if your own drama consumes your attention.

Kids will accept advice, confrontation, or discipline from someone who they know loves them and cares about them.

Life imitates "art," especially with kids. For example, this is why we have heard the nasty phrase "this sucks" from kids ever since Beavis and his buddy used it constantly on MTV. Comparing something or someone to oral sex is becoming an accepted part of everyday conversation. Kids think that if they heard it on a cartoon, then it's OK to say it. A few adults seem to think like this, too. What was intolerable is now tolerated simply because it was on TV.

Occasionally, we have had a foster child who was in custody because of some event such as the parents have died or are in the hospital, but even in these situations it is usually just one of the parents who is unavailable to the child. Very rarely, both parents have done a good job, but the kid just rebelled. The overwhelming majority are a direct or indirect result of choices the parents have made that have affected the child. Both parent and child must be held responsible for the choices that each make. The child is expected to be responsible for his behavior when he lives with us. Who is enforcing the expectation that all parents are to be responsible?

Not only does following God's design for a marriage and family give you the edge in keeping your family together successfully, but it's also easiest on your kids and on you. This is because God's design is clear and uncomplicated. We have seen some ridiculously complicated family situations, and this has hurt the kids. Complicated families raise confused kids.

There is a huge difference between wanting to have a baby and being ready to be a parent.

We have seen the clear differences between parents who keep their kids, and parents who have their kids taken away from them. When parents don't place a high value on their kids, the kids become the casualties of the immature priorities of the parents, and often end up away from the family and in foster care. It's so critical to kids that these differences between parents are understood, that much of the rest of this book will be dedicated to describing these differences in a way that I hope will be clear and understandable to the readers.

Chapter 3

QUOTES FROM THE KIDS

Here are samples of some quotes from our kids. Some might make you laugh and some may make you sad. Some are wise, but lots of them are just funny quotes from kids who don't intend to be funny, or dumb quotes from kids who think they're being smart. I've commented or explained the context in some cases, but I've let others speak for themselves. As you read, just think: soon these kids will be turned loose to drive, vote, serve on juries, and make more babies!

"I don't have any homework, because all I have is tests tomorrow."

"I don't want a husband, because I would have to be faithful."

"The mafia is not at all like it shows on TV!" Said angrily by a girl whose parents were involved with the Chicago mafia, and whose prostitute mother had died of AIDS.

"The teacher assigned us all boyfriends today!" The teacher had boys and girls pair up for an assignment.

"I'll get a job, but I won't flip burgers." He couldn't find a job.

"If they roll their eyes or say something I don't like, I just have to hit them."

"I skipped class because she wasn't teaching me anything."

"At least I looked good." She was grounded for changing clothes at a school dance in order to dress like a whore.

"We are having a pervert convention!" Said to a new resident; it was supposed to be pervert PREVENTION class. I resisted saying, "No, that's when your family visits."

"You aren't my parents; I only listen to them!" But you're here because you DIDN'T.

"But I didn't have to go to the bathroom then." I know, I know, but they're 16-year-olds!

"Who's making dinner?" This question was asked by EVERY kid as I picked them up from school one day, and told them that Debbie had been in an accident and was seeing a doctor. To their credit, most of them first asked about Debbie and the car. The dinner question was last.

"I have the biggest chest in the 8th grade!" This was bragging by a 16-year-old girl, playing her game of "I can take your man." She didn't mention she also had the most STDs (sexually transmitted diseases) in the 8th grade.

"NASA is sending a probe to explore Uranus." Don't read this one too loud. This was a boy reading his homework out loud, working on a current event project for school. Sounds like wasted tax money, to me.

"It's not the truth, but it's not a lie." Sounds like a future lawyer or politician.

"That's just your opinion." This was referring to a Bible quote. (The 10 opinions?)

"Dating an older man shows that I'm mature." No, it shows he is a baby- raping pervert.

"Age ain't nuthin' but a number." Life imitates "art" No, she didn't have a dad at home.

"It's your fault for making me mad, so it's not my fault for what I did when I was mad." Reserve a prison cell for him.

"It's your fault that I forgot, because you forgot to remind me." Maybe our sign should say "Law School" instead of "New Life Youth Home."

"It doesn't matter; I'll be 18!" A few months later from the same girl: "I hate being 18!"

"I don't need to learn manners or grammar. I already know everything I need to know!"

"We don't need to practice! We won!"

"I won't be good as long as I'm here, but I'll be good if I get to go home." She wasn't.

"Music don't affect me." She's a pregnant, unmarried teenager, and her cell phone ring is a nasty rap "song" about a "ho", (that means "whore" in English.)

"I just listen for the music; I don't listen to the words." But you have them memorized.

"TV and commercials don't affect me." But you want to dress like the girls on the video.

"So what? They're famous!" Said about another entertainer getting arrested.

"I didn't steal it, I was just borrowing it." (Or took it, or I was holding it for them.)

"I didn't vandalize anything; I just broke into it and tore it up."

"My boyfriend hasn't been in prison, just jail, so it's OK."

"She said I was small, so I had to get it out to show her." He had exposed himself to our girls to prove that he was a man. Maybe she meant his brain was small.

"I had sex with him because he told me to." This is about a guy that lived with her mom.

"I want my baby to be a girl, because a boy will grow up to hit his mother."

"It's OK; they're under the sheets." This was said while watching a sex scene on TV. I guess there are no consequences to promiscuous sex as long as no one can clearly see your skin.

"It's OK to say that word because we're just quoting a song." "Art" again.

"I have a right to watch whatever I want on TV. I'll kick in your TV just like I did at my last foster home!"

"I don't need to finish school; I'll just have a baby and get on welfare like my mom."

"I don't need to learn to work; I'll just have a man take care of me. I'll have maids."

"If my baby kicks me, I hit it back. Nobody kicks me!" She said about being pregnant.

"When we go canoeing, nobody better get my hair wet!" A dumb thing to say near boys.

"He was bad to his other girlfriends, but he will change for me."

In court: "I didn't steal that bike." DA: "Why was it in your closet?" "I found it." DA: "Where?" "In the yard of the boy that owned it." I didn't know whether to laugh or throw up.

"I know how to get back at my parents. I'll get pregnant by a black boy!" This was a white girl, upset because her dad had abused her, but that she was the one who was sent away.

"I know whose bike that is; I stole it from them!" Said while the police donated the bikes.

"My mom introduced me to her friend. We all got drunk together. I woke up naked next to him in the morning. My mom came up to me and said, 'It was good, wasn't it!' " (Eewww!)

"I'm not promiscuous. I've only had sex with seven guys!" Later, she had an STD.

"My family fights with knives. I know where the knives are here."

"Lincoln freed the slaves, but here we still have to do chores."

"When I'm 18, I can do whatever I want!" Later: "The only good thing about being 18 is staying up as late as I want."

"But if I buy it on credit, I can have it now."

"I'm already grown. I've had a baby; that makes me a woman." Someone else cares for it.

"She can't come in behind me!" This is about another girl dating her ex-boyfriend. Kids make rules too! Apparently, no one that you know can ever date any of your ex-boyfriends.

"If I talk good or use manners, my friends say I am acting white and I'm a sellout."

"My teacher has a smart mouth!" Me: What did she say? "To open my books and work!"

"I don't eat that; I don't like it!" Always said about something they have never tasted.

"But the whole purpose of a sleepover is to sneak boys in!" After she got "busted."

"I want to make my own mistakes, not learn from someone else." She was unmarried and pregnant at 19. A huge omission in her idea is that her bad decisions affect other lives forever.

"My boyfriend will help me take care of the baby, even if we aren't together anymore."

"He wants sex, so he must love me."

"The way you get to know someone is to have sex with them."

"Will you keep my kids while I travel with the carnival?"

"My cell phone bill is so high because my friends won't quit calling me."

"I can predict the future! I have PMS!" She said loudly near a family at the playground.

"But you know how it is when you are in a fight and someone puts a gun in your hand!" This was said by a boy out on bond for attempted murder, and trying to date one of our girls.

"I can't go to school because I can't read."

"I never want to see my family again!" Always followed later by: "You're keeping me from my family!"

"Isn't my mom coming? She always comes to see me when I do this!" (threaten suicide).

To the coach: "Tell me whether I'm going to play tonight, so I'll know if I should come."

"The coach should just appreciate me and be happy with how good I already am!"

"I asked my caseworker to move me because I can't make you do what I want."

"I just assumed that you wanted sex because I've never known a man who was nice to me who didn't, including my step dads."

"I can drive real good, except when I have to turn."

"When I have a job, I'm too tired for anything; and when I don't then I'm too broke." 18!

"It's because I'm black, right?" Happily, we have heard this from only of our girls.

"I'm just trying to prove that I'm not a lesbian like my mom." (She had sex at school.)

"I don't want to see my mom. She is going through a lesbian stage, right now. She's nasty and she embarrasses me!"

"I can remember being born."

"If you let a centipede count your teeth, you'll die!"

"I didn't tell what she was doing;" (run off with three boys) " I wanted to be her friend."

"I just lied and told them, (at school), that you abused girls here, so that my caseworker would move me to another place. I just wanted to go to a different school. Nobody at Dyersburg liked me; they said I'm a fake!"

"I just told them you abused me so that you would know that if you ever did, I'd tell."

"When I grow up, I'm gonna buy this place and change the rules."

"You eat cow meat?" "Where do you think hamburgers come from?" "From the store!"

"I just play basketball so everyone will look at me."

"You just don't know what it's like to be a kid. You don't understand."

"I just want to be a normal kid." Translation: not in foster care, or with foster care rules. We try to assure them that they are normal kids, but are temporarily in an abnormal situation.

"I just need someone to make a big deal over me on my birthday." We had her 19th birthday at our house because her mom was in jail, and her dad has nothing to do with her.

"I want to have a baby, but still go out with my friends. My mom will take care of it."

"No one else will have me." She said this to her mom about inter racial dating.

"Nigga is not the same as nigger, so it's OK for us to say it." An excuse by a black boy.

"I've been good here for a long time, so now I can go back home and be bad again."

To the judge: "You aren't putting me on house arrest!" He was right; he was committed.

"But I love him!" We hear a lot of this. Two of the most memorable examples are:

1. When she was placed in foster care, he still visited her family, and now has her sister pregnant.

2. He asked her to meet him at the dance, but showed up with another girl and was kissing her.

Both of these girls still considered him to be her boyfriend, and were mad only at the other girl.

"If I can't use the phone right now, I'll kill your dog!" He also threatened the staff's kids.

"Nice guys are boring. I want that 'thug lovin', a 'playa', someone dangerous."

"I'm not going to get married, but I am going to have kids. I want a baby, not a husband."

"But eating healthy food makes me sick."

"I don't want to marry him; he wouldn't be a good husband. He's too immature and spoiled. But I know he'll be a good father."

"This time, I made him promise that if he kicks me out, he'll give me 30 days to find a place first." She and her three kids had moved in with her boyfriend. She didn't get the 30 days.

"I'm very mature for my age." Almost every girl that we have had will say this, and if there is any proof, it is that an older "man" had sex with her or that she already has a baby.

"Will you loan me money for breast implants, or co-sign a loan for it?" No. By the way, what does the bank use for collateral in this case?

"Will you bail me out of jail?" No, but we will visit, if we can.

"I'm just stealing money to give to my mom."

"If I move in with him, then I can see if I like him, or leave without getting a divorce."

"I don't use the bathroom; I wait until I go to the pool."

"If she gets pregnant and asks for money, I'll just hit her. She knew what she was doing."

"I've got everyone afraid of me!"

"I want to have a baby with each one of my boyfriends."

"He abused me, so why am I the one sent away from home? Mom chose him over me!"

"I will never have sex again! Having a baby hurts too much!" She said this after the first of her three kids.

"They said I was afraid to do it!" This was after skipping band to have oral sex in a barn.

"It doesn't matter if I don't do the best I can or follow directions. I don't feel like it."

"Flappy ears." This was an answer to an oral quiz about the results of incest.

"I can't believe I gave all that up for you; it wasn't worth it." To the boy after her 1st sex.

"I want to go and give my mom another chance for us to be a family." This is what most kids who turn 18 with us, or who have been adopted by someone else, say to us. Each one who has tried has been disappointed. Mom is still self-absorbed.

"I moved in with him because he can't afford to divorce his wife; he just got out of jail."

"I wish my mom would check my homework and make me do it, like you do here."

"I need to go back into the store. I still have money left!" A future in congress!

"It's OK; he's my cousin!" I had confronted her for a boy feeling her breasts at the pool.

"I have never had a dad, before. You are the closest I have ever had to having a dad."

"These are the best grades I have ever made! I didn't know I could do this!"

"Eighty dollars is a good price for a pair of jeans!"

"I don't want to depend on my baby's daddy, or have to get money from him. He says he is paying the mother of his other baby. I'm doing OK on my own." This is from a girl who gets government housing and health insurance, plus food stamps and WIC (Women, Infants, and Children) food. Apparently, having tax payers pay your bills qualifies as being on your own.

"Just because I have his baby doesn't mean I want to be with him; he's too annoying."

"I don't like being an adult. When I was at the Youth Home I didn't have a care in the world. Now I have all kinds of things to worry about."

"All my mom cares about is herself. She gets jealous when anyone else gets the attention."

"I don't want to be a skank like my family."

"I know he doesn't have an STD."

"This is the best cooking I have had anywhere. Ms. Debbie should write a cookbook."

"If you think I'm not wearing enough, then don't look!"

"It just happened; I don't know how." This was the explanation of a girl who had sex with an older man while visiting her mom for the weekend. He had been ordered to stay away from her because of a previous sexual relationship. She had called him to tell him when she would be home and to pick her up after her mom was asleep. She had gone with him in his car to a secluded place, had gotten into the back seat, and they were kissing and feeling on each other.

"It's OK. She's just drunk." This was as they were stepping over their mom, as she lay flat on the living room floor. The kids left with me for day camp. She wasn't aware of anything.

"My sisters just got put in foster care! Can they please come and live with me here?"

"Was I as bad as my stepson, when I was there? If so, I'm sorry. He drives me crazy!"

"When I talk to the other girls here, it makes me appreciate my parents. At least my parents are married and I know they love me. I had it good at home."

"My mom told me if I didn't like it here, to allege child abuse, so I'm alleging!" This was a-10- year old boy, who was mad at me about not letting him be the pitcher for our baseball team. Children don't use words like allege unless taught to do so.

"My mom didn't leave us alone with no food. When the caseworker came, my mom was out getting some food for us."   The problem is, mom never came back.

"You gotta have fun sometime!"   This was a girl who had left the hotel to get high with three strangers while on a school trip. Now 19, she is in jail for meth and has an STD. More fun!

"It's OK to lie, but only to get something you want; you can't expect kids to be honest."

"It's not working out with my family. Can I come back?"

"It was self-defense!" This was from a girl who had gotten angry at another girl on the school bus, had chased her off of the bus, into the school, down a hallway, and into a classroom in order to hit her.

"The only reason he can't take me out anywhere in public is because his ex-girlfriend would get mad that he treats me better than her treated her. She's just jealous that I have him!"

"Stupid cow!"   This came out of the mouth of a boy who had grabbed the rope that was around a cow that had gotten loose. He refused to let go as the cow bolted and dragged him through our yard, a small stream, the garden and a nearby field.   At least he finally let go when the cow ran through the cactus fence. The rest of us didn't think it was the cow that was stupid.

"I don't want to leave here. I'd have to buy my own shoes!"

"The only reason my mom hangs out at the bar so much is so that she can win money playing pool to buy us some food."

"My mom just brings me to the bar with her so I can drive her home." This girl is fourteen.

"Mr. Mark, you're too bold! I'm afraid someday that somebody is gonna shoot you for what you say!"

"Your marriage is like a fantasy. I've never seen one that good before."

"Are you saying that if you had the chance to have sex with a good looking 15 year-old-girl, that you actually wouldn't do it?" (Yes, that's what I was saying!) A few years later, he told me "My wife and I got divorced because she wouldn't stay in her own bed!"

"I know how to get extra presents. Have your boyfriend give you your birthday present early. Then break up with him just before your birthday and go with another boy right away, so he has to get you a birthday present, too!"

"You can't expect teenagers to be honest! It's OK to lie if you have a reason. I only lie to you when I don't want you to know the truth." This girl gets upset when her mom lies to her.

"Mr. Mark, how does Ms. Debbie put up with you? You're so worrisome!"

"I don't need to go to church. I know everything about God, already"

Chapter 4

MOST OF US KNOW THIS ALREADY

Here are a few of the more memorable gems of wisdom that we have actually had to say to our kids. Many of these are in here just for fun. Others make me wonder if the child may have learned these basics if the parents weren't gone, in jail, too busy, or high on something. Parents, if your teenager acts like he is smarter than you, you might feel better if you read a few of these.

When you jump in the river, close your mouth BEFORE you hit the water.

To find the right guy, you have to be the right girl. Would he be looking for one like you?

If you don't want to marry an alcoholic, don't date guys that you met at a bar.

Never iron your clothes while you are wearing them.

Pull up your pants. No one wants to see your thong or your "plumber imitation."

Closing your eyes won't keep the softball from hitting you.

If you can't swim, don't jump off the diving board.

You can't call yourself a dad if all you did was get the girl pregnant.

If he wants sex before marriage, then it can't be love.

The rear-view mirror is not just to check your makeup.

Don't stand neck deep in the wave pool if you can't swim.

Don't date a guy who abused his other girlfriends or cheated on his wife to be with you.

Your teacher told you ahead of time about a test so that you can get ready for it.

Put your canoe paddle down inside of the canoe, not out in the current of the river.

If you aren't a whore, don't dress or talk like a whore, or date a guy who wants a whore.

You can't answer the questions at the end of the chapter until you've read the chapter.

If you make the same decision as before, you can't expect it to turn out better than before.

There is such a thing as right and wrong. If you think that I am wrong for saying this then you have proved my point. People who say there is no right or wrong still believe they are right.

Don't put empty pitchers back in the refrigerator.

Bending over and rubbing your backside against his crotch doesn't qualify as dancing.

It is impossible to simultaneously move your glove to the ball and your body away from it.

Don't jump in the river wearing your backpack, especially when it's carrying your lunch.

Don't have sex until you're ready to have a baby. You aren't ready until you're married.

You can't lay a hot iron down on the carpet.

You won't get credit for your homework unless you turn it in.

Denying reality won't make it go away, but it makes you look like an idiot.

Being a man is not about age or getting a girl pregnant. Real men can make themselves wait for sex, consider consequences, think unselfishly, and take responsibility for their actions.

Never do cartwheels in the shower.

Decisions have consequences. If you can't face the consequence, don't make the choice.

To get a good job, you need to learn the actual English language. Nobody will offer to pay you a lot if you talk like you ain't got no learnin.'

Gangs are for punks and losers who are too afraid to walk down the street on their own.

Never carry a crab in your pocket.

You can't play shortstop in your hiking boots.

A quarter of an hour is not 25 minutes.

Don't call me at home and ask me where I am.

"The best defense is a good offense" works in football, not when you're driving in traffic.

Never jump on the bed when the ceiling fan is on.

Never aim your sled toward a utility pole.

It's not wise to blow your nose with your mouth open.

It's not easy to get a glue-type mouse trap out of your hair.

Never flush an ink pen down the toilet. It clogs up the toilet, and you still don't get out of doing your homework.

Never try to cover up a hickey by placing a hot curling iron over the spot on your neck.

Never try a running slam dunk off of a picnic table.

When you jump off of a diving board, jump forward, not straight up.

Don't expect a boy to do a man's job. If he wasn't man enough to marry you before he asked for sex, then don't expect him to be man enough to stay around, support you and the baby, and be a good dad if he gets you pregnant. Be prepared to go to court to get child support.

If you don't want your kids in foster care, make better choices than made by your parents.

Following God's standards won't keep you from pleasure; it provides pleasure while protecting you from pain. Would someone who sacrificed for you not want you to have pleasure?

Chapter 5

THE NUT DOESN'T FALL
VERY FAR FROM THE TREE

Here are some of the statements the parents of our kids have made to the court, the children, or to us. They cover the range between the silly and the ridiculous. Parents: if you recognize yourself in these statements, please recognize the damage you are doing to your child and get help. For all of us: we have to recognize the damage that the culture of irresponsibility is inflicting on our kids, our families, and our society. Then each of us must insist on personal responsibility from everyone from our leaders to our teenagers because the damage is to all of us.

Of course, there have been many wise and positive messages from the parents over the years, but I have chosen to highlight the statements that shows the philosophies of life and parenting that leads to having your child placed in foster care. Some of these are quotes and some are not direct quotes, but are accurate with the point. I have commented after some of them, and have let others speak for themselves. Warning: these have been known to cause sickness or disgust. Some of them would be funny if they didn't have such an affect on our kids.

"My kids don't need a dad." You did such a good job by yourself that your kids are living with us. What your kids don't need is any more brothers or sisters until you and dad get it right.

"I don't give her medicine to her when she's with me. She says she doesn't need it."

"I let her have sex in my house because I would rather her have sex here where it is safe." Safe from what? You don't allow STDs in your house? Her daughter ended up pregnant and abandoned by the boy.

"I let her do her drugs in my house where it's safe."

When mom was called from school and told that her 10-year old had brought a gun to school, she replied that it was OK because it was just her old gun and she still had her new one at home. When he came to us, we searched his bags thoroughly; I wouldn't want him to bring her new gun.

"If you don't like it there, allege child abuse on them."

"Run away."

To child: "I need you back home _____."
(Fill in the blank)
    A. "To protect me"
    B. "To take care of me."
    C. "To take care of the other kids."
    D. "To get a job and pay the bills."
    E. "So I can get your check."
    F. "To take care of the house for me."
    G. All of above

A black mother from Memphis told us, "That's how black boys are; they fight, cuss, and hit women, so he shouldn't get disciplined for that from the school or from you." This excuse was used after her son had hit another boy at school, and had fought with the teachers who pulled him away. All three of her sons were with us awhile. Later, after he returned home to live with his mom, this same boy beat up his girlfriend. I wonder if mom made excuses for that, too.

A black mother from Dyersburg told us, "That's how all black girls are. They have sex with a lot of boys and they get pregnant. You have to expect it. That's what I did." Her daughter already had a baby at home, which was being cared for by the great grandmother. Mom was telling us not to make a big deal of the fact that her daughter had offered sex to a boy here and given him a pair of her underwear so he wouldn't forget.

"I give her cigarettes so she won't use drugs." It doesn't work.

A grandmother of two of our kids had offered to sell the boy and girl to a neighbor man.

"I want my kids to think I'm cool." or "I just want to be my daughter's friend." It's pretty cool that your kids live with us now.

"The_____(fill in the blank) just doesn't like me or my kids."
  A. Judge
  B. Teacher
  C. Principal
  D. Police
  E. Probation Officer
  F. All of above

"What should I put here where it asks why you weren't in school?" He had been out to attend a funeral. Our staff couldn't resist and said, "The truth would work!" The mom thought for a second and said, "That's right! We could just put the truth this time!"

"It's the school's fault he failed; they kept suspending him!"

To child: "Don't listen to anyone or let anyone tell you what to do!" Including you?

To son: "Be a man! Don't let anyone tell you what to do, especially your mom!"

To daughter: "If someone tells you what to do, you just hit 'em! You're not a slave!"

"She did just fine when she was home this weekend." Mom would tell us this when she brought the girl back, but it was a complete lie. Later, when the girl went home and disobeyed, mom asked, "What makes her think I'm going to let her do that?" Mom sent her back to us.

"No interracial dating!" said the white dad who married a Korean woman, and the Jewish mom who married a Japanese man. I'll see if I can find a Japanese Jewish guy for your daughter.

A mom reported that the boy's dad was dead so she could get his social security. The dad was alive, but her son was already upset because she had told him that his dad was dead.

A number of moms have lied to our kids about who is the biological father.

"I can't come to see you unless you give me money."

"I don't have a ride or the gas to come to see you." Later, the kids find out that mom had a ride and enough money to go to Mississippi to gamble or across the state to visit someone else.

"I don't visit you because it upsets me to see you there." It's still all about you, isn't it?

"When my (pretty, 17-year-old) daughter is home, my (much younger) boyfriend baby sits her for me. They like to go out riding together."

"I broke up with my boyfriend and moved out, but my daughter still lives there with him."

"When you are 18, you need to quit school and sell crack with me."

"I give in to her just to get her to be quiet." This is one reason you need a father at home.

"It's easier to just do it myself than to teach her to do it and get her to do it."

39

"I never graduated, so my kid doesn't need to, either."

"I can't get her to go to school."

"It's not his fault he wouldn't go to school. They wouldn't teach him anything."

"Without my kid's check, I'm going to have to go out and get a job."

"This family doesn't have a problem; she does!" Oh, I thought your daughter was part of your family.

"I drink and do drugs because my kids stress me out."

We have had many moms who have chosen abusive boyfriends or husbands over their own daughters. They have said so in court, when they refuse to move out or kick the abuser out in order to have their daughter home with them. If he had sex with her daughter or beat her daughter, it was the daughters' fault, according to mom. The mom stays with the rapist; the girl stays here with us.

"We all let my daughters find our boyfriends for us!" This was a mom who, along with an aunt and the grandma, had sexual relations with the men who were dating her daughters.

"I knew Sheria was your daughter; she looks just like Debbie!" I love this; she's adopted!

"Just give me some money, then and everything would be OK!" Said by an abusive junkie mom who had lost all of her kids, after her DCS (Department of Children's Services) caseworker showed her what she could do in order to have her kids back home.

(Laughing) "All of my kids have been suspended from school this week for fighting! They are just like their mom!" Said as she was elbowing and winking at her kids.

"My kid shouldn't have to work." Obviously, you feel the same way about yourself.

"Nobody but me can discipline my kid!" This includes us and the school. She never does.

"My kid says she didn't do it, so she didn't!" We all would like to believe our kids.

Parents promise to come for a visit or take the kid for a weekend or holiday, but don't show up

"I leave the discipline up to their mother." It works so well, your girl lives with us, now.

Parents have threatened our staff, DCS, or school staff in front of the kids.

"Then I will just leave, since you don't want me here!" We had a baseball team of our boys, and I was the manager. This was a dad who was watching. He had yelled an instruction to his son which had conflicted with mine, confused the boy, and caused the boy to be put out. I had told the dad that we appreciate him coming, and would he please encourage the boy, but let me coach third base. His wife apologized for the fit he threw in front of his son.

"We don't sell 24x20 air filters; all we have is 20x24." This was a mom who worked at a home improvement store where I shop. I told her that it was OK because I could turn it sideways.

We have parents of our girls who tell the girl that they want her home and will do what they need to do to get her home. Then they tell us, the DCS, or the court, that they don't want her home. One said, "I just told her that I wanted her home so she wouldn't get mad at me."

"Why don't you make good grades like this at home?" Mom + dad = better grades.

"If she keeps disrespecting me like this, then I'm going to stop lying to cover up for her."

"She loves Mountain Dew! She drank a whole 24-pack on her (24-hour) home pass." Of course, she felt sick and couldn't sleep when she returned from the day with mom.

"I don't know where his clothes are. He loses them every time he comes home for the weekend!" Let's see, could it have anything to do with having a twin brother at home?

"I don't know how my cigarettes and lighter got in my son's pocket!"

"My daughter is not ever coming back to my house, again!" Parents, be careful what you say when you are angry. This was a 16-year old girl with unresolved emotional problems, but you don't turn your child out of your home forever. Tough love is good, but forever is way too long.

"I need her home with me, because I just can't sleep without her lying in bed next to me." She was referring to her 17-year old daughter, who said she was promiscuous in order to prove that she wasn't bisexual like her mom.

"Will you take all of my kids for awhile?"

MORE STORIES

I take a lot of pictures of the kids, and we have more than two dozen albums full of them. Going through the albums makes me smile, and also jump-starts my memory and gives me ideas for stories to tell you. Many of our pictures are from trips we have taken with our kids, and one of our favorite trips is to the Smoky Mountains. At night, the kids love to go into Pigeon Forge and race go-carts (so do I!), so we have lots of pictures of kids on go-carts.

One year, I had a brilliant idea about how to get awesome go cart pictures that didn't look like all the rest: we would ride in the double carts, so I could be copilot for one of the girls and take close-up pictures of the other girls while we raced. In the first race, I found it impossible to turn around in my seat to get a good shot, and when the girls were ahead of us, all I could see was the backs of their heads. So before the next race, I said, "This time, when you're next to us or if we are passing each other, turn and look at me and smile so I can get a good picture." (OK, it doesn't sound so smart as you're reading this.) The girls actually listened, and it started out OK as I took pictures while we bounced, slid, and crashed around the track until C and B came up next to us. C was driving, and came up on my right, so she could pose with a big smile for an action close-up. B was intent on staring forward and screaming. Just as I lined up the picture, my chauffeur, Sheria, made a hard left turn to stay on the race course. C didn't. Now, I've seen and have even been in some go cart crashes that are worthy of war stories in my time, but nothing like this one. They T-boned the guardrail at full speed, and the cart bounced straight backward into the oncoming traffic. Their necks snapped forward and then backward as they bounced off the guard rail, followed by a series of slams from the carts coming up behind them as they eventually slid to a violent stop. Plus, I didn't even get a good picture!

As we walked back to the line after the race, C and B were greeted by the kids in line with "Awesome crash!", "Cool!," and "Did that hurt?," or "Weren't you the ones who wiped out into the rail?" The boys who worked at the track walked up and asked if they were OK, because that was the best crash they had seen all summer. Then, they gave C and B free rides for the rest of the night. I'm not sure if they felt sorry for them or wanted to see if they would do it again. I put my camera away for the night.

C went on a trip to camp with the Young Life Club. She had worked and saved her money to help pay for camp and for spending, and she planned to have some money left when she came back. However, she was completely broke when she came home to us, and told us that she had saved some money to bring home, but something had happened. On the trip back, the bus stopped for a break at a convenience store in C's home town. C had seen her aunt there, who quickly left to get C's mom, because mom never came here to visit her daughter, and rarely even called. At first, C was exited to have a brief, rare visit with her mom, until she realized mom's reason for coming with her aunt. Mom asked her if she had any money, and could mom have it? Of course, C gave her mom all the money she had left. Mom still didn't come to visit after that.

MJ couldn't wait for the "freedom" that she would have away from our rules. She did keep her waitress job when she left. Her unemployed boyfriend would take her to work and then wait at a table until she had earned enough tips, so he could take her money and spend it while she was working. Seeing this, the restaurant owner told him that he couldn't hang around anymore, and that he needed to leave so MJ could do her job. He responded by saying that he would make MJ quit her job. If he couldn't be there, then he wouldn't bring her to work. She married him.

Mary and Michelle are sisters who were with us together. It was December, and part of our Christmas here is to help out at the Mission. We packed and passed out boxes of food and toys to give to families, and helped the Mission help others. Ruth was a widow and the hard working manager of the Mission store. She never relaxed until everything was done, and expected those around her to do the same. Roy was a man who lived at the Mission, and who helped out where he was needed for his room and board. He had been working closely alongside our kids for a couple of days. One day at supper, I kept hearing Mary and Michelle refer to something that Ms. Ruth's husband had said or done. Now, I knew that Ruth was a widow, and so if these girls had seen and talked with her husband recently, Ruth would surely like to know about it. When I asked the girls who they were talking about when they referred to Ruth's husband, they described Roy. I told them that Ruth was a widow and that Roy was just helping her, like we were doing. Thinking about picking on Roy and Ruth, I asked, "What made you two think that Roy was Ruth's husband?" They both answered, "Because she's always telling him what to do!" No, this isn't what they see in our marriage, but it may be part of the reason that their mom couldn't keep a man around. I wonder if these girls are married now.

Like many of our girls who don't have close relationships with their dads, SL had an older boyfriend back home, and he wasn't allowed to contact her here. Usually in this situation, if we make it hard enough for the "man" to have access to our girl, he will quickly move on to another girl who isn't so well guarded. However, nobody else would have Randy, so he kept trying to get to SL, and she was flattered. This loser used the common trick of picking her up at school, and for this he spent a weekend in jail, and was put on probation and under a court order to stay away from her. When SL first heard about his consequences, she cried and was upset with me, but this didn't last long. This guy soon moved in with a 30-something-year-old woman and her 13-year-old daughter, and got both of them pregnant. Even SL was disgusted. She is married with kids of her own now, and we enjoy an occasional talk with her. Randy continued to harass her when she became an adult, and even after she was married. She is happy that we did what was right, and didn't let her do what she thought she wanted at the time. Girls usually change with the passing of time. Perverts usually don't.

AL turned 18 in March of her senior year of high school, and quit school the next day. She could have stayed with us until she graduated, but a couple of more months of school were just too much. She had a couple of thousand dollars saved up from her job, which her boyfriend's family spent in just a few weeks. The boy didn't give here anything but a baby, and AL's life has been a complicated struggle since then. It is the rare child who has the wisdom and character strength to be on their own and make good decisions at 18. Even kids who have been nurtured in good families may be ready for mom and dad to send them to college, but aren't yet ready for complete independence. Foster kids have the opportunity for support and services after 18, and some take advantage of this. Many, however, decide that 18 is a magic number, and that no help is worth being held accountable to someone else. By the time they are wise enough to realize their mistakes and get help, the cycle has usually extended to another generation of kids.

Our four eighth graders wanted a graduation dance, but the school didn't sponsor a dance for the occasion. The "gang of four" approached me with the news that there was going to be a dance, even if the school didn't sponsor one. It was being organized by some classmates and they wanted to go. My answer was, "You can't go to a dance unless it is supervised by the school, or unless I'm there to chaperone it!" Since I knew that they wouldn't want me anywhere near their dance, I thought that this was the end of the subject. That is, until a couple of days later. The procedure after school at the K through 8 School was to park, go into the office, and have your kids paged to come out of class to go home. As I was walking through the parking lot, a mother called to me, "I wasn't going to let my daughter go to the dance, until I saw that you were sponsoring it. Now I know it'll be safe!" She got into her car before I could think of an answer, and another mom said in passing, "I see you're sponsoring the dance. Good luck!" As soon as I stepped into the office, the secretary said, "I'm so glad you're sponsoring the dance; a lot of parents who weren't going to let their kids go are now going to let them!"

I was finally able to respond with, "What are you talking about?"

"The 8th grade dance!"

"What dance?"

"It's on the signs all over the school! I'll show you!"

As we walked into the hall, a teacher said, "That's so nice of you!" And sure enough, there were handmade posters up and down the hallway advertising the 8th grade dance that was sponsored by Mark and Debbie Loftin and another couple who must have been tricked in the same way. It was too late now, and besides I had said, "Unless I'm there!" So we were there. I spent most of my time slow dancing with Debbie and stopping to move the boys' hands up off of the girls' pants and back up onto their backs. One boy, who was 16 and the only one who drove himself to 8th grade, finally gave up and left. I didn't miss him, and after all, other parents had depended on me.

We try to give the kids some regular exercise, and this includes riding bikes. Usually, we go to an area near our house at the edge of town which includes our fairgrounds and National Guard parking lot. During one bike ride, a boy, JB, talked a girl, FW, into having some quick sex on the sidewalk outside behind the National Guard building. Another girl, FE, was with them and was supposed to be watching out for me. After they were caught (JB had bragged), I confronted FW about this, and asked why she wanted to do this, especially outside and in front of someone else. She said, "Because he told me to!" FE, who was 16 like FW and already had a child, told the group, "I wouldn't put my naked butt down on that cold sidewalk for nobody!" Well, at least she has some kind of standards and a little self-respect. JB did us all a favor and ran away when confronted. He's not enough of a man to face consequences. He was caught soon and locked up.

Shortly after this, I was checking the kids' rooms, which is part of my daily routine here, and found a pair of FE's underwear in a boy's drawer. Now, you need to get the picture: FE weighed nearly 300 pounds, and this was not a sweet little silky bikini from the mall. It was a big ol' pair of "granny panties" from the discount store. Thankfully, they looked fresh out of the package, and not fresh off of her super-sized derriere. Naturally, I asked the boy, "What is this doing here?" He answered, "She gave them to me and I didn't know what else to do with them." FE told me, "I just wanted him to remember me." Maybe he was too afraid to say "No, thanks."

A number of our kids have been diagnosed with asthma before they come to stay with us. Most of them no longer have a problem with it, once they are here. This is because they aren't in a house or riding in a car full of cigarette smoke, like they were at home. One of our boys still used and carried an inhaler, but he would "lose" it whenever he went home to his family for the weekend. After having to replace it a couple of times, he finally told us what was really happening. His dad had asthma, too and would take his son's inhaler, use it, and keep it for himself. He told the boy that we could get him another inhaler. Don't have kids if you're selfish.

Chapter 6

THE DIFFERENCE

For the purpose of the observations in this chapter, I will define an unsuccessful parent as a parent who has had his/her child or children removed from his/her care and custody into foster care, detention, or some type of treatment facility. Successful parents will be defined as parents who have not had a child removed from their care or custody. A successful parent may have placed their own child into some type of treatment. (Seeing and meeting a need is a sign of being a good parent.) We have had many opportunities to know and work with both kinds of families, so these observations aren't just theory or out of a textbook. They are from real life. These opportunities have included the programs that I mentioned in the introduction of this book:

Crusader Youth Outreach

Camp Hickory

New Horizons Youth Ministries

Cedar Ridge Children's Home, and

New Life Youth Home.

We have also observed kids and families among our own family, and by being involved with:

Coaching or managing kid's baseball and softball

Big Brother and Big Sister program volunteers

AWANA club, as volunteers

Helping with other Mission programs, such as the day camp and day trips with local kids

Volunteer youth sponsors at our church for over 15 years, and

Serving as band parents and on various committees for our local schools, including the Truancy Board and the Discipline Hearing Authority.

Of course, the obvious differences between successful and unsuccessful families are that the unsuccessful families abuse, neglect, or abandon their kids, and successful families nurture their kids. There would be no point to this chapter if this was all I had to say, since this is already well known and documented. I wouldn't waste my time or yours if I didn't have something to add to the obvious. In our work we've made other observations that may not be as obvious, but are also crucial for a successful family. I need to share these with you, in the hope that there will be fewer kids removed from their families. Having watched successful and unsuccessful families for over twenty years, we've confirmed the following observations.

If you want to be a successful parent, don't:

Have kids before or outside of a marriage. Temporary relationships make troubled kids.

Neglect, abandon, or abuse your marriage partner. This is at least as critical with your husband or wife as it is with your kids. Kids who aren't certain that their parents love each other and will always be together can't be certain that their parents love them or will always be there for them.

Abuse alcohol or drugs. Don't be drunk or stoned around your kids.

Give up on your relationship with your kids or marriage partner. Divorce must be rare, and only for such extreme circumstances as unfaithfulness, abuse of the kids or partner, or abandonment.

Expect your kids to meet your needs.

Expect or force your kids to be what you wanted to be. Don't live vicariously through them.

Be afraid to make your kids unhappy with you for doing the right thing; you aren't elected so you aren't in it for the approval rating.

Get into competition with each other.

Use the TV (especially music videos like on MTV or BET) to baby-sit.

Raise your kid to eat only french fries, or whatever they choose.

Encourage your kids to break the law, or break it for them, such as buying them alcohol or drugs, or letting them skip school, drive without a license, lie to get a hardship license, or use tobacco.

Make rules you can't or won't enforce.

Make promises you may not keep.

Make threats you can't or won't back up.

Make unreasonable or impossible expectations.

Shelter them from (safe) natural, logical, or legal consequences.

Call them names.

Put each other down or argue in front of the kids.

Put down other authorities in front of the kids, such as teachers or police.

Relate to others by aggression, fighting, or violence.

Forget what it's like to be a kid.

Let other parents set your standards.

Be unaware of who their friends are, especially boyfriends, or where they spend their time.

Make excuses or blame the kids, your spouse, the government, racism, your parents, your job, or anything else for the choices you make or for the consequences of those choices.

Allow your kids to be manipulators, especially when they try to manipulate mom versus dad.

Think things make up for time. It doesn't work, and bribes like this teach kids manipulation.

Allow your kids to be "latchkey kids."

Go in debt to buy something the kids want but don't need. Set this example in your own life, too.

Allow your daughter to dress like a whore. Don't dress like a whore yourself.

Act like you are entitled to whatever you want. This includes entertainment choices for all of you.

Deny or cover for them; get angry with the police, judge, teacher or principal when your child has done something wrong. Don't assume your child "didn't do it" before you get the facts.

Show disrespect for those in authority over you.

Be a drama queen or let your daughter ascend the drama throne.

Sleep around, or allow your boyfriend/girlfriend or your daughter's boyfriend to sleep over.

Be promiscuous, or teach your daughter to get things with sex, or your son to get sex with things.

Be unfaithful to your husband or wife.

Have children with anyone except for your husband or wife.

Punish all the kids for the behavior of one of them.

Punish when you are angry or have lost control of yourself.

Be too lazy to work, and expect the government to take care of you.

Be a hypocrite.

Pretend to be a good parent in public, but don't live it out at home.

Expect your parents, your older kids, the school, or the courts, to do your job to raise your kids.

Argue or fight with your child.

Teach your child to listen to you only when you scream or get angry.

Try to be the child's friend or peer by trying to be "cool."

If you want to be a successful parent, do:

Get married first, stay married, and be faithful to your husband or wife. This is absolutely critical! For your kids, there is no substitute for depending on your healthy, committed marriage.

Be honest with each other and your kids.

Work with each other, never against each other. Discuss differences away from the kids.

Be dependable, to each other and to the kids

Show love to each other. Know what makes your partner and your kids feel loved.

Be a consistent example of strong moral character, model, and leader.

Put your kid's needs above your wants.

Build character in your child through chores and responsibilities.

Know Christ and live as though you do. Your faith must be more than just words or rituals.

Be involved in a church, not just a member. Have family devotions and pray with your child.

Pray for your child.

Have fun together.

Spend quantity time. Quality time comes as a result of quantity time, and can't just be scheduled.

Look for and take opportunities to give sincere, specific praise, recognition, and affection.

Be supportive and encouraging with each other and the kids. Look for the positive.

Be a dependable provider for your family. Sacrifice things you want for yourself, but not time.

Discipline your child, making the expectations clear, consistent, fair, and reasonable.

Consequences for disobedience need to be as immediate, just, age appropriate, and as natural as possible. Discipline needs to "fit the crime," and is for teaching. It's never for revenge.

Spend time sharing the interests and activities of each other and the kids.

Communicate. Know how each other communicates. Listen.

Expect your kids to be responsible for their actions and words.

Accept responsibility. Have your actions match your words.

Take pictures. Use them; don't just leave them on a disc or in a box. Keep mementoes, albums, or scrapbooks, and hang family photos in the house.

Tell family stories and keep family traditions.

Teach your children that to abuse a privilege is to lose a privilege.

Eat meals together. Turn off the TV during meals. Sitting with your family while you talk on the phone doesn't count as being together.

Teach and model good manners. Expect your kids to try new things and to eat healthy meals.

Monitor their entertainment, especially the TV and music. Monitor your own, too.

Know your kids' friends and their parents.

Know where your child is, what he is doing, and with whom. This is much easier if you do things together, or if you have your kid's friends join you on activities or at your house sometimes.

Model respect for authority and laws, including how to deal with injustice or disagreements.

Model and expect self-control.

Be involved in the education of your child, whether it's home school, private, or public school. Check homework. Know the teachers. Don't attend just ball games; attend teacher's meetings. Chaperone trips and dances. Join or sponsor organizations or clubs and volunteer to help.

Love each other and your kids unconditionally. Love the sinner; hate the sin.

Admit your mistakes and explain the consequences that have resulted from the mistakes.

Apologize if you are wrong.

Demonstrate the proper priorities in life: First, your relationships: God, your husband or wife, your kids, your extended family, friends, and community. Second: your activities: Your church and ministry or service to others, and your job. Your job is a means to an end, not the end itself.

One or both parents have a job.

Pay your bills.

Model contributing to your community, country, society, and church. Expect your kids to follow.

Honor and value your marriage and each other.

Recognize sexual predators and protect your kids from them.

Give your kids some power to make decisions as they mature and develop character and wisdom.

Give your young children a childhood, without the stress or responsibilities that will come later.

Support each other emotionally. As the kids say, tell each other "Don't worry, I have your back!"

Give each other the chance to spend time alone, and to spend time with individual kids.

This may not be an exhaustive list of the differences, but it is a list of clear observations we have made, contrasting the families that have their kids and the families whose kids end up in foster care. These same keys to success have also applied to our own lives, our own family, our own relationship with each other, and to the work we do with our kids at the group home. We invite you to learn from our experience. We enjoy working with kids, but we want you to keep your kids at home with you.

Chapter 7

LOOK WHAT WE HAVE DONE TO OUR KIDS

Parents, the moral choices that you make affect your kids. Dangerous moral choices on your part hurt your kids. Your kids can become casualties of your decisions. Twisted choices twist your kids' minds. Selfish or immature decisions that you make will seem normal to your kids, and so your kids will repeat your mistakes unless you honestly acknowledge and accept responsibility for your mistakes and for the consequences.

Based upon our observations, this chapter is a description of the consequences of poor morals and poor decisions of the parents in the lives of our kids. In particular, this is what can happen to your kids if you weren't married, got divorced, had an affair, live together without the security and commitment of marriage, the relationship between mom and dad has ended, there is incest, or the father is no longer in the home. Troubled relationships produce troubled kids. None of our kids have had each of these traits, but each of our kids has had some of these traits. You may recognize some of these as typical teenage traits, and some of them are, but we see that these traits are taken to the extreme and last much longer with foster kids. I've made no attempt to list these traits in any particular order, but all of them are typical enough for us to observe them in many of our kids. Here are some common consequences in kids of harmful parenting:

Physical, sexual, and all other kinds of abuse by mom's boyfriends or other husbands.

Attention seeking behavior, including at school. With girls, this will include seeking attention from boys and men, and becoming "drama queens." If mom has a new guy, the kids may compete with her for his attention and affection.

Poor impulse control.

Insecurities, untrusting, stressed, nervous, or always worried.

Guilt, or thinking "Something must be wrong with me," or "It's my fault."

Depression (not just sadness, but also professionally diagnosed).

Favoritism; kids may favor one parent and parents may favor certain kids, including treating kids from different dads in different ways.

Kids who think of the dad as the "Fairy Godfather," who in real life or in fantasy shows up to rescue them from mom, bring gifts, or whisk them away to a magic place of toys and no rules.

Hatred toward dad, distrustful of men.

Disrespectful of adults or authority in general.

Manipulative, selfish, or arrogant. Manipulations include pitting mom against dad.

Kids who think that if you have to have a job, then the government has failed you.

Angry. Some can identify only what makes them mad, not what makes them happy.

Anger is the only emotion they can easily express.

Aggressive or cruel. This can be physically or verbally. We see kids with an extremely cruel sense of humor, for whom the only thing that seems to be funny is the pain of others. They will laugh at handicapped people, or watch sporting events in the hope that someone will get hurt.

Passive, allowing others to take advantage of them.

Hypersensitive to real or imagined slights.

Poor self- image. "Even my dad doesn't care about me."

Don't fit in with mom or dad's new partner, live-in, or family. "He has another family."

Fantasies about whichever parent they are not living with or never see.

Unfair with or resentful toward one parent, while idealizing the other.

Problems with denial; unable or unwilling to face or accept reality.

Poor view of marriage and low expectations of marriage.

Confused about what defines a family, or who is the actual dad, or who is related to them.

Believe that love is conditional and temporary.

Not nurtured. They may have missed part of childhood by assuming adult responsibilities.

Can't bond with others, and often sabotage relationships.

Unstable. This may include an inability to handle frustration or change.

Can't commit; think that if there is a problem, you run away or quit. Don't finish things.

Drug and alcohol abuse.

Promiscuity and attraction to older partners. Girls don't realize they are looking for a dad.

Sexual identity confusion; some may believe that they are homosexual, but they are really missing and looking for the love, affection and attention that they need from mom or dad. Some moms have raised their daughters, and even their sons, to hate men. This can then cause sexual identity confusion, or even denial of how you biologically, naturally, and obviously are created.

Easy prey for sexual predators and easily fooled by smooth talkers.

Boys don't know how to be real men or how to treat women with respect. Girls don't know how to respect themselves, so they use sex or skimpy clothes to attract male attention.

Bullying others, or the opposite extreme of having a victim mentality. (Sometimes one child will display both of these traits.)

Overly critical of others.

Have very poor heroes or role models, mostly coming from the entertainment industry.

Low achievers, low expectations, and not taking advantage of talents, ability, or potential.

Performance at school is below capability and this is often related to poor behavior.

Suicide talk or threats of violence toward others.

False or greatly exaggerated accusations of mistreatment from others, or threats to make such accusations. Habitual complaining about real or imagined mistreatment by others.

Problems with authority, authority figures, rules, or laws. They are not used to male authority in the home and so may react poorly to it at school. They aren't used to obeying their single mom, and so are disdainful of any female authority. They will treat adult women as peers.

Unable to relate to adults in a positive way. Avoid adult interaction. "Us against them."

Girls try to create their own families by getting pregnant as soon as possible, and don't expect the boys to commit or help. After all, her dad didn't help her mom or stay with her.

Attracted to gangs or other poor peer groups.

Don't feel valued or loved by one or both parents.

Negative attitude, pessimistic, cynical, and hopeless. They look for the negative and would rather choose to whine or complain about something than work to accomplish a change.

Behavior that shows psychological issues, such as cutting themselves, or eating disorders.

Role reversal. An attempt by the child to take on an adult role in the family, such as parenting or protecting the mom or other kids, or having an incestuous relationship with the dad or father substitute. This may begin when the parent allows the child the treat adults as peers, or when the parent chooses to try to be a friend to the children instead of an authority. This also is most likely to happen when one parent leaves, or with children of alcoholics or drug abusers.

Refusal to take responsibility, and playing the victim, including when something is clearly a direct consequence or their own choices.

Bitterness, often shown by rejecting others before others have a chance to reject them. A feeling of rejection by one or both parents is too bitter, so they refuse to be the rejected one again.

Others can go in the extreme opposite direction, and become people pleasers. This has a nice sound, and they are more pleasant than the bitter kids, but they often put themselves at risk in order to please others. They may not even know who they are or what they like to do. They are afraid to disappoint or say no to others, and hope that they can repair the family by being good. These kids can be a pleasure to have around, but they're at great risk to be sexual abuse victims.

Some of our kids just don't seem to be "wired" right. A certain stimulus will evoke a different, irrational, unreasonable, or unpredictable response from them than it would from "normal" well-adjusted person.

Immature for their age, with poor social or coping skills.

Diagnosis of an emotional disturbance.

An imaginary life. This is one of the most painful traits to watch, and puts the child at great risk of abuse or ridicule. Some examples include girls who pretend and tell others that a certain boy is her boyfriend and that they have done physical things together. The boy, however, will never call, and when he is inevitably asked about her, won't even know her or will barely be acquainted with her. Other girls have pretended that "popular" kids are their close friends or relatives, and that they are very involved in each other's lives. Kids who simply know about someone, or know only their name, may pretend to know them well. Sometimes the reality of the biological family life of our kids is so bad that they pretend to take on the life of someone else, and that whatever happens to this other person has happened to them.

These are the results we see in the lives of kids when one of the parents (and it has almost always been dad) is gone. I'm not talking about when dad is temporarily gone, such as for his job or if he is serving in the military. I'm talking about when he is out of the house or out of the child's life for good. He may be in jail, may have left mom, or maybe he hasn't even ever acknowledged that he has a child, or mom may have never been honest about who is the dad. Whatever the situation, something important is missing from the life of a child, and we have observed the consequences in the lives of the kids. There is an old myth that says when dad leaves, it will make the kids, especially boys, tougher and more able to handle adversity. This may work in western movies or in music, but not in the real world. In the real world, kids need a dad.

Parents, don't try to give me that tired, old "It's my life" line. It's your kid's life, too. If you make immoral or immature choices, then your family and your kids will be the casualties. If you buy a product that needs assembly, but ignore the maker's design, instructions and warnings, then you will assemble something that doesn't work, or is dangerous. Those who make war on the family by ignoring, altering, or replacing the design, instructions, and warnings from our Maker make casualties of our kids.

What can we do to keep more of our kids from becoming casualties of the battle for the family? I believe that the first thing we need to do is to call off the war against the family in our culture, society, and our nation. Those who have waged war on the family by polluting it, trying to redefine it, or by working to destroy it need to face the damage that they have done to our kids and to our culture. The ideal answer is for those who war against the family to honestly realize their mistake and accept responsibility for the damage, so that we can declare peace and work together to restore the family before it's too late for our nation.

Secondly, we as individuals must each recognize the damage that we have caused or allowed, and then commit to making individual choices that protect our families, kids, and society. This means that we must make wise moral choices in our relationships, marriages, and sexuality. We can rebuild the building block of our society one person, one family, and one child at a time if each of us will make choices with the future and our kids in mind. This way we can prevent any more of our kids from being casualties. For individuals who refuse to take these steps, we need to begin approving, implementing, and enforcing some of the ideas I will present in chapter 14.

Chapter 8

ENGLISH-TO-TEENAGE
DICTIONARY

Here is my handy guide for parents or anyone who is required to communicate with teens. I won't cover slang terms because they come and go, but I will give you a few actual English words that you may think you understand. It is crucial, however, to remember that when these words come out of a teenager's mouth, they will have entirely different meanings than the meanings you learned in school. Some have multiple meanings. Refer to this guide whenever your kid says, "You just don't understand!" Feel free to make copies and carry this around with you or put it up on the refrigerator to use until you become fluent. To clarify your understanding, I have used some of them in sentences. I cannot guarantee these definitions because your teenager will change the meanings at any time for his convenience and to keep you confused.

Abuse 1. Anything you say, do, or don't do that I don't like. 2. Not letting me do whatever I want whenever I want. 3. Telling me no. 4. Not giving me special preference.

Accept Be completely OK with anything I choose, do, or say. Never give advice, warnings, or disapproval in any manner. Example: "Why don't you just accept me as I am?" may mean "Don't take the car away just because I'm failing in school ever since I've had my license."

Forgive 1. Whatever I did, you must never mention it, and you may never let any previous choice that I have made effect my freedom. 2. No repentance required on my part, and no consequences for my behavior.

Freedom Anything I want to do without ever any consequences or responsibility on my part, plus the parents are required to pay for it. Example: "I can't wait to get my freedom!" may mean: "I can't wait for you to pay for me to go to college and have no idea what I'm doing there"

Freedom of speech Anything I want to say, anytime, anywhere, any volume, to anyone.

Going out (dating) Talking on the phone, writing notes to each other at school, text messaging or e-mailing, or acting possessive. Note: never actually going out anywhere.

Grown (mature) 1. I want something. 2. I have lived a certain number of years. 3. I don't want to listen to you. 4. I have done something that I should have waited to do until adulthood.

Hollering (yelling) 1. anything you say that I don't like or want to hear. 2. You didn't say it sweetly, meekly, and gently enough for my hyper-sensitive ego, so I get to play the victim.

Love 1. A crush or attraction . 2. Sex or lust. 3. A temporary feeling; something you can "fall in and out of." 4. Overpowering hormone attack. 4. A word used to talk a girl into bed.

Over protective 1. any curfew, or any expectations that I need to be supervised. 2. Any restrictions on dating, choice of entertainment, or where I spend the night. Example: "Kids with overprotective parents go wild when they turn 18" may mean, "I want to get pregnant by a 30-year-old crack-head thug immediately, and not wait until I am 18, because he won't wait 3 years!"

Privacy Never watch me, know or ask what I am doing, check on me, be in my room, or know who I am with or with whom I am talking.   (See trust)

Respect/Disrespect   1. Acknowledge my superior intellect, position, and dominance over you. 2. You must talk nicely to me, but I can be rude to you. (Respect only goes one way: from you to me, and never from me to you.) 3. Allow me to be rude and aggressive to you. If you respond firmly, then you have disrespected me and I get to act indignant. If you respond gently, then you are too weak to deserve respect. Example: "I respect my mom." means " I will be hostile to you if you talk about my mom, but I will also hit her, curse her, and disobey her."

Rights   Anything I want to have or anything I see someone else get to do, and my parents or the government are required to pay for it or provide it for me, immediately.

Slavery   Anything that I am asked to do, that I don't feel like doing at the moment.

Success   1. Being famous, and it doesn't matter why. 2. Showing off. 3. Possessions or "bling." 4. Being on TV, in the movies, or in a video. 5. Getting away with everything I do or say.

Trust   Never asking, checking, or knowing what I'm doing, even if I have recently or habitually acted untrustworthy. Example: "You don't trust me!" (Usually either accompanied by crying or spoken with shock) may mean "I don't want you to know I'm dating a married man."

Whore   Female definitions: 1. A girl who wants to have sex with or have a baby with the same boy with whom I want to have sex or have a baby. 2. Any girl who attracts the attention of a boy who I like. 3. Any sexually active girl, except for me.   Male definitions: 1. A girl who has had sex with other boys but will not have sex with me. 2. A girl who has had sex with me, and with whom I am no longer "in love" or interested, usually due to the fact that she already consented to have sex with me or says that she is pregnant with my child.

Hint: If your teenagers use one of these words or phrases, then take out this list and read them the definition. This will accomplish two things: It will impress them with your multilingual skills, and it will deny them one of their favorite means of manipulation.

Bonus Section: Female Teenager-to-English Phrase Translation

Here are some phrases which are most often used by teenagers of the female variety, with an attempt to translate so that parents, particularly of the male variety, can understand. Caution: Some females who are no longer teenagers may continue to use these phrases in order to confuse you. I will not include some of the already well-known trap phrases, such as, "Does this make my butt look big?" or "My hair looks awful today!." If you don't know how to avoid responding to these already, my advice is to stay a safe distance from females, especially of the teenage variety.

"I'm ready to go." means that I have decided to go, but I need to change clothes, do my hair and makeup, pick out some shoes, do my nails, and find my purse.

"I don't care." means that I care very much, but I won't tell you so you have to guess what I want, and you should know me well enough by now to read my mind. Example: She may say, "I don't care where you take me to dinner." If you make a suggestion but don't guess correctly, she will say, "No, I don't want to go there." Your natural response will be to point out that she obviously does care where you take her to dinner, but now you have attempted to use logic with a teenage girl. You should know better.

"I wouldn't go out with that ugly boy!" means he hasn't asked her or he has dumped her.

"Its my life and my body and I can do what I want with it!" means that she wants to be able to follow any impulse, but if there are any consequences for these impulses, then you and the government must be responsible to pay medical bills, child care, or any other kind of expenses.

"Its none of anyone else's business what I do." (see above) means only until I need help, such as with bills or caring for my child. I am entitled to taxpayer help, without any taxpayer comment. It's the taxpayer's business to pay any expenses for what I do, but it's taxation without representation. It will be someone's business to care for my child, but nobody can tell me to wait until I am married and ready to parent a child before I get pregnant.

"I don't care what you get me for my birthday." means that you are expected to read my mind and that this had better be amazing.

Chapter 9

THE FUN, THE JOY, AND
THE REWARD

A residential ministry is not just about the drama that surrounds you when you live in a home full of hormone controlled, impulsive, needy, delusional, know-it-all kids. We also have some fun. There are joys, pleasant surprises, and rewards. Here are some of them:

The privilege of fighting on the front line as a warrior in the battle for kids, families, and values.

The opportunity to be used to make a positive difference in the lives of kids and their families.

Watching and helping kids enjoy new experiences. I love it when they discover something or find out that they can do something, or when they realize that they are somebody and can succeed.

Seeing God work in their lives, and the joy of demonstrating God's love through us to others.

Seeing and celebrating progress and growth, and watching the kids recognize these in themselves.

Participating in major events in their lives and celebrating milestones, such as getting a driver's license, birthdays, a first paycheck, proms and graduations, a first date, or making the team.

A big Christmas every year.

Kids who keep in touch and keep us part of their lives after they leave, or when they are adults.

Racing go carts, playing paint ball and laser tag, going to the beach, ball games, a theme park or the Smoky Mountains and countless other places, and this is just when I'm working.

I can wear what I want and don't have to commute to work.

Seeing lots of stupid or silly stuff that I can record forever in this book.

Watching families re-build relationships and reunite, or watching kids find an adoptive family.

The opportunity to recognize the most common causes of foster care, the chance to share these observations publicly, and maybe to help reduce the number of kids coming into foster care.

Working closely with Debbie. You didn't read this to hear about us; I may have to write a sequel.

Tamara and Sheria, who are our adopted daughters. Maybe I can brag about them in my next book, too.

Real Christianity is taking care of "orphans and widows in their distress" and we are blessed for it.

Chapter 10

MAYBE YOU CAN DO IT, TOO

Debbie and I have two adopted daughters, Tamara and Sheria. They are biological sisters, and we are committed to them forever. Forever started over six years ago, when they first came to live with us, and the bond will never end. Melissa came to our home when she was 14, and we were given custody of her starting the next year, until she turned 18. Others have returned to our home by choice, or have decided to stay with us beyond their 18th birthday until they were ready to be on their own. All of these kids are still "our" kids (even though they may be adults by now). Some people think we're crazy, and they're right - we're crazy about our kids! I know that couples are often afraid to adopt teenagers, but I would like to ask those of you with good, strong marriages and morals to think about adopting or taking custody of an older child. Here are some reasons to think about adopting teenagers:

You have the chance to get to know and love them before you commit to them. You don't have to guess or wonder about their personalities.

They are already potty trained and don't spit up on you.

They can sleep through the night. (Through the day, too, if you let them.)

They can articulate what they want, instead of just cry.

You choose each other. You know it's what the kids want, too. You get to hear them tell the judge, and lots of other people, that they want you to be their parents. (You may want to record this for later!)

They don't need to be carried, and can carry their own stuff when you go somewhere.

They can wipe their own nose.

They are capable of cleaning up after themselves.

They are immediately capable of recognizing and returning your love.

There is no hospital bill to adopt foster kids, and they already have their shots.

There is no waiting list for teenagers. There are waiting lists for parents, instead.

You will be meeting a need, and you can translate your beliefs into actions.

They can be realistic about their biological parents. We recommend an open adoption.

They can get a job soon, or maybe get married and move out soon.

You might get grandkids sooner. Debbie will show you a picture of Alydia, if you ask.

These additional reasons to adopt are reasons for all ages, not just for adopting teenagers:

You can blame genetics if they act stupid, or if you have to go to a meeting with the teacher or to traffic court with them. They can't blame your genes if they get pimples or gain weight.

Husbands: You don't have to wait two months for sex with your wife after an adoption, and your wife will never scream, "You'll never touch me again!" during an adoption ceremony.

You are less likely to faint during an adoption ceremony than while watching your wife give birth.

Wives: You can keep your figure, and you will still be able to fit into your clothes.

Strangers won't try to pat your belly, give you advice, or tell you horror stories about childbirth.

You are imitating God when you adopt, such as where He says that He offers to adopt us as His children. He says He likes it when we imitate Him!

STILL MORE STORIES

Kids of all of the races who live in our area have lived at the group home with us, and sometimes we get some funny looks or questions when we're in public together. Some people assume that I am a coach with my ball team, or a church youth worker with the youth group. (I have been both.) Others can't resist asking, "Is she your daughter?" and this is usually when I have a black girl with me. We like to have some fun with these situations, so if Debbie isn't with me, I sometimes answer, "Yes, but she looks a lot more like her mother." The girls try not to laugh, and the questioner never knows what to say to this. I love their expressions, though.

KT and LS both played basketball for the middle school. KT is a tall white girl who was the leading rebounder. LS is a short black boy who could steal the ball better than anyone else on the team. It was Homecoming and all of the players were being recognized at the high school. In such situations, our kids have the choice of announcing the names of their biological parents or our names, or both. KT and LS both chose to use our names, solely, so in front of the crowd, a tall white girl was introduced as the daughter of Mark and Debbie Loftin, and a short black boy was introduced as our son. I think we were the proudest parents in the gym.

Two sisters, T and NW, had just moved in. They had left an abusive situation, and we were still getting to know each other. One evening at supper in our dining room, one of the sisters spilled her drink. Both girls jumped up from the table, scrambled to separate corners of the room, and cowered down in the corners with their arms covering their heads. Both were screaming, "I'm sorry! I'm sorry!" Nobody else moved for a few seconds and the other kids were just looking wide-eyed at the sisters and then at us. I just calmly said, "It's no big deal. Just get a rag and clean it up." The sisters whimpered for a few seconds, and then uncovered their faces and looked at each other and then at us. Debbie got up to help clean up the mess, and dinner and the normal conversation resumed. A few weeks later, the mom decided that she wanted the girls back with her, so whenever she would visit, she would inspect them for cuts or bruises and throw a fit as she pretended to find something. After all, if abuse was the reason they were removed from her, she should be able to get them back by accusing their caretakers of abuse.

Among our kids at the group home, there is a special group that stands out from the rest. This group includes the kids who have lived with us the longest, or who chose to stay with us beyond their 18th birthday, in order to graduate or accomplish some goal which would better prepare them to be on their own, such as building up a savings account. This group also includes one girl who was removed from state custody into our personal custody, and the two sisters whom Debbie and I have adopted. If I define this special group to include those who lived with us for three years or more, then the group would number only around twelve kids. There are many others who stand out in our memories with whom we have had unusually good relationships. The reasons for these relationships include kids who openly appreciated us for what we were doing, kids who have kept in touch with us regularly since leaving, and kids who had little or no relationship with their biological parents, and who have chosen us to be the parent figures in their lives. There are dozens of these kids, out of the more that two hundred who have been here. I will not even attempt to name them all, because I would surely leave out someone accidentally. The twelve or so that I mentioned first stand out because there is simply no substitute for time in building close relationships. This is a critical point for parents to grasp. My next few stories will be about some of the kids in this special group.

Melissa knew that she may not be protected or provided for if she returned home to her mom, and wanted to be sure that she would not be forced to return home until she was ready and had chosen to do so. Most abused, abandoned, or neglected kids, understandably and naturally, tend to imagine that everything will be much better when they are back with their families than it was when they were previously together. This, unfortunately, is only the reality when the parents are available, willing, able, unselfish, and honest enough to do whatever it takes to change the home environment and habits that caused the kids to be removed. Melissa had an unusual grasp of reality and did not fantasize about how good it would be if she were with her mom again. All of the children in the family had been removed, and as it is with too many of our kids, mom was unwilling to make the changes needed to get her kids back and keep them.

Melissa had a talk with her state caseworker, and was told that as long as she was in state custody, the goal for her would be to return home someday. However, she was told, if someone else had legal custody of her, then returning home would not have to be the goal. All four of us together made the choice for Debbie and me to ask for custody of Melissa, since she had been here nearly two years already, was nearly 16, and since Debbie and I both loved her. The judge agreed, and she was here two more years. The summer after she turned 18, she moved in with her mom to have a chance to be a family again, but that lasted only three weeks before she called us to ask if we would come to get her. Melissa had matured some, but mom had not. Melissa stayed a little while, and returned again for awhile after her divorce. Though custody ended at 18, she is still one who is like a daughter to us, and we are proud of how she is doing now. Mom still hasn't changed.

Jon moved in with us as a 16-year-old 8th grader. Like most foster kids, he was behind his age group in school. This is often because the parents have moved so often or have no permanent address, or simply don't require their kids to go to school. Jon's dad had died, and his mom would never have any of her kids back. He was with us nearly four years, and we were proud of him for choosing to stay in school and graduate at age 20. He was also on the wrestling team for three years. For the last few months of school, he had moved into his own room at the Mission in order to have some independence. One of the most common excuses for not staying in school until graduation that we hear is that they don't want to be 19 or 20 when they graduate. The fact that they choose to ignore, though, is that the other option is to be 19 or 20 and not graduated.

According to our girls, the crowning of Miss DHS (Dyersburg High School) is the biggest social event of the high school year. Sheria was a freshman cheerleader in '02 and was honored by being elected to the Miss DHS court. There is a dance after the ceremony, and the tradition is for the dance to begin with a father-daughter dance in the middle of the dance floor, for all of the girls on the court. So I enjoyed a dance with Sheria. Later in the spring when the yearbook arrived, I was stopped by the principal as I entered the school. He commented on the great picture in the year-book. Someone in the office said the same thing. I didn't know what they meant until I picked up a copy, and sure enough, there on page 36 was a half-page picture of two father-daughter couples dancing to "My Girl," along with the caption, "Daddy's little girl." We were one of the couples! So now there is a big picture in the year-book of me dancing with one of the two prettiest girls in the whole school (Tamara was the other prettiest girl in the school). That's something that never happened to me when I was in high school.

Among the traditional events during high school homecoming week were the powder puff football games between the classes. Tamara is our athlete, and during her junior year she played softball and basketball, plus ran for the cross country team. Known to be fast and aggressive, she was chosen to be the quarterback for the powder puff game for her class. She had never thrown a football, so we practiced together in the front yard until she could throw an accurate spiral. She didn't need much of this new skill during the game, though, because she ran for two touchdowns for the winning team. That's something else that never happened to me in high school.

There are more than five acres here, and we have always had some animals living here. There have been dogs, cats, cows, horses, chickens, and hamsters. Like other families, we keep them as pets, but we also use them to help teach responsibility and how much is involved in caring for other living beings. Occasionally this responsibility has included searching for a missing cow or dog. On one such occasion we were looking for our dog, Deacon, who had been reported to be in a nearby neighborhood. As I drove through the neighborhood, the girls walked around the houses to look for the dog or knocked on doors to ask about him. Holly and Angel walked into an open but dark double garage that was attached to a house. Since they could barely see, they flipped a switch on the back wall to turn on the light. But it wasn't the light; it was the garage door opener. Instead of flipping the switch again, they just screamed as they watched the door close and take away the remaining light. The owner of the house heard an awful scream coming from his garage, and opened the door from the house. This caused more screaming, until he flipped the light switch to expose two hysterical girls. When they gathered their senses enough to explain, he laughed and opened the door for them. I was glad to know that the adventure ended well, and I was also glad to explain to him that I was not biologically responsible for these girls. We never found Deacon, and he was one of many dogs missing from our neighborhood that day.

One of my favorite places is the Smoky Mountains, and one of my favorite things to do there is to visit Cade's Cove. I have seen wild turkey, bear, and lots of deer there. The deer are relatively fearless, because there has not been any hunting there for many decades, and they are used to seeing humans. On one trip, we had seen a herd of deer in an open area and had gotten out of the van for a closer look. I had instructed the kids to be very quiet, and to move very slowly so we could get close to the deer. There were a handful of other tourists with us, and one of the men coaxed a doe close enough to eat from his hand. Now, I will try to say this next part gently and with class. As we were quietly admiring some of God's most beautiful and graceful creatures I was proud of how quiet and respectful our kids were acting. No one made a noise. That is, until TC broke loose some gas from her bowels that I would estimate to have at least a seventy or eighty decibel level. The rest of us humans tried not to laugh out loud, and to distance ourselves from TC, but it was too late. The entire herd reacted to the noise like it was a cannon; their heads came up, their white tails came up, and they bolted into the brush at full speed. Everyone looked at TC and burst out laughing. With all the planning it takes for a vacation, you just can't plan a memory like that. If TC insists on denying this incident, I will stop using just her initials.

Holly was 17, and had been with is for a year when her sisters, Tamara and Sheria, joined her here in our home. Tamara was 14; Sheria was 12. As soon as Holly had found out that her sisters had also been placed in foster care, she asked us if we would take them, and we were happy to reunite all three sisters here. Putting families back together is one of our priorities. Unlike her sisters, Holly wasn't available for adoption, and she was an adult before we were able to adopt Tamara and Sheria, but we love her and consider Holly "ours" anyway.

Chapter 11

SINCE YOU ASKED

People we meet are often curious about the kind of life we live at a group home for teens. We get a lot of questions, and we are happy to answer them. We also get some comments that are funny or reveal some common misconceptions about this kind of work. I won't cover all of them in this chapter, but I am including some of the most common or some of my favorite questions or comments from "civilians". Then, since I wrote this book, I get the last word.

"How are you funded?" At New Life Youth Home, where we have been since 1987, we are a ministry of the Dyersburg-Dyer County Union Mission. The Mission owns the home and pays our bills. For the kids in state custody, the Mission receives a payment similar to what a foster family would receive. Whatever expenses that the foster payment will not cover are subsidized by the Mission. In addition to subsidizing the amount of money we need, the Mission provides the money when we need it, instead of waiting for the state payment to arrive. If you are thinking of this kind of work, you need to understand two financial facts. One is that foster care payments do not cover all of the expenses for the children, so you can't make a profit if you intend to meet the needs of the kids. The second is that you cannot depend upon when the money will come from the state, but you will have expenses for the children as soon as they come to you.

"Do you have normal teenagers?" I was a teenager once, and have been working with them since I was nineteen. I still don't know what a normal teenager is. I'm not sure the words "normal" and "teenager" should even be close together in the same sentence. What we do have are teenagers who behave in manners that are typical or common for kids in their situations. The typical issues with acceptance and self-image are taken to the extreme because our teens often aren't sure of the love of both parents, and then assume that other kids will look down on them.

"How can you stand a house full of other people's teenagers? I had two of my own and I couldn't stand to be around them most of the time." I usually just laugh at this one.

"Do you have racial issues in your house?" Almost never, but a few of the parents have had this issue. It has been helpful to have people of other races on staff with us.

"Do your kids fight each other?" Very rarely, and any fights are usually between siblings.

"What is the hardest thing about what you do?" Listening to constant lies, especially when the kids lie about us or make false accusations about us. If you want to do this kind of work, know that it is a matter of when and how often, not a matter of if this will ever happen.

"Do you get attached to them?" "Do you miss them when they go?" "How do you ever give them up?" Yes, because this is about relationships. What helps is to keep in touch with them, and because you get so busy with the next one. If you don't want to give them up, adopt!

"Are you successful?" That depends on your definition of success. The kids get great care and usually thrive here, but it will take years to know if the cycle of bad choices is broken.

"What are the biggest frustrations in your work?" To see kids who have made a decision to change their lives, and make great progress here, go home and sink down to the lower level of expectations that their parents have or allow for them. Two examples are particularly saddening. One is that when they were here, they recognized the need for God's help, but at home they are not involved in a church where they are nurtured, so they don't continue to grow. The other is when they make poor choices in men and morals, and so repeat the cycle that their mom started.

"What do you do or how do you feel if they mess up?" This may sound cold, but to keep going I have to remind myself that they have messed up their lives, not mine. We are responsible to the families, our community, and to God to do our best; the kids are responsible for their choices. No matter what choices they make, we like to keep a relationship with them.

"What is your saddest story?" The mother of one of our boys surprised us with a visit a couple of years after he went home. When he was here, he was stubborn and put up a cocky front. She was distraught because he had died in a car accident a number of months before her visit here. She was hoping for some assurance that he was in heaven. She asked Debbie if he had ever made a decision for Christ while he was here, and Debbie had to be honest and say that, to her knowledge, he had not. Parents, if something is important to you, don't put off talking about it with your kids.

"Why are you so strict? You're kids are so good!" Just turn this around for the answer.

"It must be very rewarding." Yes, but maybe not in the way that you would expect. You can't depend on kids to accept what you teach, meet any of your needs, or be appreciative to you.

"I have a real job. I don't just sit around with a bunch of kids watching TV." This is from a conversation with a man who worked at Captain D's. Now, I've done fast food work and it is honest, hard work, but he doesn't live with all of his teenage workers 24/7 at the restaurant.

"You have a good program here! I like the small size with the homey, family atmosphere. I could help you get a government grant so you could bigger." Yes, this was from a government worker. He was a mid-level bureaucrat. It's nice to be recognized for doing good work, but how could we waste the taxpayer's money to ruin the small size that gives us the family atmosphere?

"We know that the church-sponsored homes do a better job than our own group homes, and do it for less money." This was the same state worker who made the previous statement. I need to be fair and give him credit for his wisdom and honesty, since I picked on him before.

"I wish this other child I know could be there with you," or "I'm so glad she's with you now." This kind of comment almost always comes from a teacher. Teachers are often the first ones to spot behavior problems from the child that indicate problems in the child's home.

"Are most of your kids abused by their parents?" Some have been abused or neglected by the biological parents, but abuse or neglect is much more likely when a parent has a partner living in the home who is not the biological parent or who is not married to the biological parent. The reason is that these partners are often not invested in or committed to providing for the needs of the kids or protecting the kids.

"You should write a book!" You should buy my book! You should buy it for everyone on your Christmas list. You should give it to someone else to read when you're done. You should make sure your local library has it. You should see that your legislator reads it. Seriously, you should know the reason we have so many kids in foster care and help do something about it.

Chapter 12

WAIT!

I've never known an expectant or new mother who hoped that her baby would someday live in foster care. I've certainly never had a girl in foster care who hoped that her child would also live in a foster or group home, someday, just like mom. What I have seen, too often, are kids who come into foster care because their parents weren't ready to have a child and to be a parent.

Sadly, I've also seen too many girls in foster care who are blindly repeating the same choices that were made by their mother, and so put themselves and their children at risk of being separated someday. One of my goals in my work and in this book is to help end this cycle in as many families as possible, so I'm including some observations about being ready to be a parent. I won't waste your time by just repeating the standard advice. I'd like to give you some things to think about and some questions to ask yourself. I'd like to see these questions included in pre-marital counseling, and in counseling for unwed mothers. For your kid's sake, wait to have a baby until:

You are MARRIED, permanently and faithfully. Anyone who is too immature or selfish to commit to a marriage for life is too immature and selfish to have a child, which is also a commitment for the rest of your life. Remember, you will give birth to a person, not just a baby. It takes a mother and a father to make the baby, and common sense and human history say that it takes both parents, living together in a healthy marriage, to meet the needs of a child. This is how we were designed to nurture a child who will thrive.

You have the self-esteem and brains to refuse to be just another one of his "baby mamas."

You are ready for drastic changes. Properly caring for a baby will take over your life.

You have finished school.

You can afford the expense. This includes being able to quit or take off work, have a budget worked out, and have enough money saved so the family can live on one salary for awhile.

You are at least 20, and have not just grown older, but have grown up. You need some time in between being a child and having a child. You may succeed if the mother is only 18 or 19, but only as long as you are married, unusually mature, both of you have finished school, and if he has a good enough job and income to support three people.

You are unselfish enough with your time and money to put the baby's needs before yours.

You are healthy and clean from drugs. You can go for years without drinking or smoking.

You are finished partying or going out with your friends to places where a baby can't go.

Both parents want kids and are ready for one of you to stay home for awhile and both of you to change your lifestyle in order to care for the baby.

You know if he has any other kids, and how he takes care of them and their mom, and why he is not with them now. If you are the reason he is not there, then get away from him now!

You have the time, patience, and emotional stability.

You have the character strength to set a good moral example for and discipline the child.

You have child care planned and budgeted. A good plan is for mom to stay home awhile.

You understand that wanting a baby isn't the same as being ready to be a parent forever.

You can change your schedule, budget, social life, and entertainment. Barney will come soon, and ball games, recitals, band concerts, school plays and such will come later.

You no longer think like a baby yourself. You've outgrown the "Its all about me" stage.

You have the character strength to make yourself do whatever is needed, even if it's hard or if you don't feel like it.

You try baby-sitting for others, and you can't give the baby back when it's screaming or needs a diaper changed, or just because you are sleepy or want to do something else.

You are mature enough to no longer act like a child, including having developed the habit of making decisions based upon wisdom and consequences, not upon emotions, lust, or impulse.

You can give up some control. The BABY decides when it's hungry or needs changing.

You are ready for the baby to be a priority, not a decoration, a doll, or a diversion.

You understand and can give unconditional love, and your own need for real love is met.

You understand that it won't just be a baby; it'll be a person who won't always be a baby. Would you like to take care of someone who acts like you, or treats you like you treat your mom?

You are ready for a lifestyle of sacrifice, not indulgence.

You understand that this will be a person with needs, not a fashion accessory that you put away when the style or season changes.

You know that a child is not a means to meet your own needs.

You are ready to sacrifice some of your identity. You will soon be known at school or the ball game as simply _____'s mom or dad.

You are ready to postpone or cancel some of your own plans or dreams.

You realize that, once you are pregnant, you may never again be able to honestly say, "It's my life and I can do what I want!" Everything you do will now affect the lives of at least two other people, and you need to be mature and unselfish enough to behave like you understand this.

You are mature enough to realize that a child is much more than just a souvenir of a past relationship. If you want a memento of your first love, then take a picture together.

If you are not ready for marriage and to raise a child, then you are also not ready for sex.

Chapter 13

YOU WILL HAVE TO EXPLAIN THIS TO YOUR KIDS, SOMEDAY

Here are some really stupid reasons or excuses that we have heard from some girls who were pregnant, were trying to get pregnant, or who thought that they wanted to be pregnant.

For revenge: revenge on a parent who ignored or abused her, revenge on a boyfriend who was unfaithful, or revenge on a girl who had gotten pregnant by a boy our girl thought was hers.

For attention: attention from her parents, her boyfriend, her friends, or from the baby.

For someone who will love me, need to be with me, or will always be mine and won't go.

To show I'm a woman, or for him to show he is a man.

So I can quit school.

So I can get welfare or child support or a free apartment.

Because my friends are pregnant or have babies.

Because I got high or drunk.

Because I forgot my pill or my birth control didn't work.

To meet any of her own needs.

Because of what he said: He told me to, he wants me to, he wants me to prove my love for him, he wants me to be his "baby mama", he wants me to have his baby just like all of his other girlfriends, or because he will love me.

Because my parents want grand-kids, or others expect it of me.

To dress it up and show it off. To play with it, buy it things, or enter it in beauty reviews.

I just like sex. I just get excited and do whatever I feel like doing. It's no big deal.

Because I just wasn't thinking, or I just don't think about that sort of thing at the time.

Because we would make a pretty baby together.

To make him stay with me, or for other girls to know that we are together.

Because even if we don't stay together, I will still have his baby and he'll help me with it.

Because I want a baby with each of my boyfriends.

Because I don't want to be the last one in my family to have a baby.

Oh, well. It just happened. I just can't control myself.

I MAY NEVER RUN OUT OF STORIES

Part of the fun in residential work is when we take the kids to places where they have never been, or give them experiences they have never had. Many of the kids in Chicago or Baltimore had never even been out of their neighborhood, much less out of the city. The Chicago kids hadn't been to the Loop, and the Baltimore boys hadn't been to an Orioles game, until we took them. Many of our kids from the Northwest Tennessee area have never been to Memphis. I get a kick out of watching city kids in the country, and watching small town kids in the city. The next couple of stories are about how tough kids act when they're out of their element.

Johnny was one of the boys who were active at the youth center where we volunteered in Chicago. His escapades in the neighborhood included stealing a police car. We did a lot of weekend camp-outs with the kids, near Princeton, Illinois. These kids had never seen real darkness before, and the only wildlife that they were used to seeing were rats and pigeons. We could keep these big-talking kids safely in the tent at night simply by confiscating one of each of their shoes and all flashlights. The darkness was just too dangerous, and besides, there were no sidewalks. We taught the kids to fish off a dock near our campsite. Getting someone like Johnny to put a worm onto a hook was funny enough, but his real fear came out when he actually landed his first fish.

He probably had never seen a fish that wasn't square and breaded, and this was an actual, live, vicious, six-inch Sunfish that was flopping on the dock! Johnny's next assignment, of course, was to get the hook out of this pond monster's mouth, so the wiggly little thing could be put into the bucket or released back into the pond. But tough guy was so absolutely petrified of the slimy little fish that he couldn't make himself touch it, much less pick it up and reach into its mouth to get the hook. The best idea he could come up with was when, under vigorous protest from the rest of us, he grabbed the fishing line a few inches above the fish and beat the fish repeatedly against the dock, making sure the little fish never touched him. In the end, the little fish looked like mashed potatoes, and Johnny didn't look very tough anymore.

TB and JT were boys from small towns in Tennessee who had never been to the city, or anywhere far from home. Every year we take our kids to Libertyland, which is a theme park in Memphis, and they were with us there one summer. I told them that the log ride was one of my favorites, and took them there, entering from a direction where you couldn't see what was happening on the ride. I rode in the back of the log so I could watch them, and besides, I knew what was about to happen. As the log gently negotiated the first few curves, they looked back at me and laughed, saying, "This is nothing!" However, as the log floated out of a tunnel and started to be pulled up onto the conveyer belt to the sky, TB looked back at me and asked, "Did you know this was going to happen?" Now it was my turn to laugh! When we got way up to the top, they looked around at the entire park, looked down the slide, and then both looked back at me with an accusatory expression. "Are we going down there?" they screamed as they pointed down the chute. I yelled, "And there ain't no turnin' back, so hold onto your glasses!" Just then, we lurched into the start of our run down the chute, with two tough boys screaming like girls the whole way down. By the time we stopped, they were laughing, and we had to go two or three more times. For the rest of the day, they made sure to look at the rides before they stepped in line.

ME was a girl who had come to us after her behavior toward the father at a potential adoptive home had cancelled the adoption. In the evening, Debbie and I were in the living room while the kids worked on homework. I was on a couch, with my back to the girls' hallway, and Debbie was reading in a chair. ME walked up behind me with a note from the teacher for us to sign. Without looking back, I reached up for the note, and told her that I also needed a pen. As I held my empty hand back to her, again without looking, she said, "Here, I have one!" But instead of putting her pen into the open palm of my hand, she pressed one of her breasts into my hand. I jerked my hand away and turned to look back at her, but she just ran down the hallway, giggling all the way. I know why the mother in the adoptive home refused to adopt her. We eventually had to move ME to an all-girl placement, because she was also propositioning the boys here. As an adult, she has had kids from various men. She is looking for the love that she never received in her family, but what she learned from her family has so twisted her idea of love, that she can't tell the real from the phony. Some of her kids are in foster care in Georgia, so the cycle continues.

In the spring of 2000, we took our girls to a Diamond Jaxx baseball game in Jackson, where some of our girls were singing the National Anthem with the church youth choir. A Chrysler dealer had a display of new cars outside the gate, and we stopped to look. Sheria and I both admired the green Sebring Convertible, which I believe is one of the best looking cars to ever come out of Detroit. I took a picture of the little, smiling, blonde-headed 13-year-old in the Sebring, with the top down, and she said it was her dream car. I put the picture in the album, and didn't think about it anymore. A couple of years later, after we had adopted Tamara and Sheria, we promised to give one of our cars to each one of them, as a high school graduation present. The gift for Tamara, who graduated in '04, was to be Debbie's car, but we agreed not to give Sheria my car when she graduated in '05, because it was a 5-speed, which she couldn't drive. I sold my car, and in the spring of '04 was looking for a replacement when I found a green, 2000 Sebring Convertible in Memphis. I'd forgotten about the day at the Diamond Jaxx and the photo of Sheria, until Angel saw my new car. She had lived with us at the time and had been to the game with us. She said, "That's just like the one in the picture!" - so we got out the old album, and sure enough, it looked just like the one in the picture of Sheria in her dream car. When Sheria graduated, we took another, matching picture of her in her gift. Yes, I sure do miss driving it, but there isn't anything that's more fun that giving your daughter one of her dreams. In our work, we've known lots of dads (and kids) who've missed out on these events and this kind of fun.

Since, like biological parents, we are expected to prepare our kids to be on their own someday, we teach independent living skills here and try to mentor those who need it from us after they are on their own. In addition to chores and skills learned here, some of the kids have been able to get jobs, bank accounts, cell phones, and driver's licenses. After they turn 18, they can also register to vote, buy cars, furniture, or put deposits on apartments or utilities, in preparation to be "launched" into the world. Usually, these are milestones that we celebrate with them, but sometimes it's been a cold-blooded, hard-hearted dose of reality. This happens when the kids find out that a parent or grandparent has "stolen" their identity. Some of their relatives have used the kids' names or Social Security numbers to get phone service or credit, get a job, or some other use. This, of course, makes it very complicated for the kids, and gets them understandably angry and frustrated. Sometimes, someone tries to collect money from the kids for the parents' bad debts. One of our girls recently had a call from a car dealer who was looking for her dad and for some money. Such a role reversal is another common trait among the families of our kids.

The boys had helped me fix up an old car. It was a '64 Mercury Comet, and it looked cool with its new chrome rims and fresh paint. I was out in the Comet, with the car full of our girls, when a car pulled up to the left of us at a red light. It was a Mustang full of teenage boys, and they were all obviously staring in our direction. The girls were looking back a little, but were also elbowing each other, smiling, and nodding their heads toward the boys. The light turned green for the turn lane that the Mustang was in, but the driver didn't go anywhere; he just kept staring at us. The girls started giggling, and I thought that I was about to get into another situation, so I rolled down the window and said to the driver of the Mustang, "You're light is green!" He answered, "Thanks! We were all just looking at that nice car. It's cool!" Then they just drove away. I had to laugh at the girls, who just said, "Oh, those boys were ugly anyway!"

SM had just returned from a weekend with his family in Baltimore, when we had a call from the house parents of the 6-to 10-year old boys' house, next door. During a visit there, SM had gathered some of the younger boys around their sandbox. He made an anatomically correct form of a woman's body out of the sand, lying in the sandbox. Next he taught a couple of the boys how to simulate having sex with the sand figure. When confronted, he told us that when he went home for weekends, he watched pornography with his uncle, and was showing the younger boys what he had seen. Naturally, this was discussed with his foster care case manager, to see if visits would be stopped, or if the uncle would be required to keep his porn away from SM. The answer was that the family had a "right" to watch porn in their home, even with kids. It's an ACLU thing, to protect the rights of perverts and pornographers, even at the expense of our kids.

JH couldn't walk very well or very far, with his cerebral palsy. He hated using a walker. When we walked into Wal Mart, he begged me to let him drive one of the electric carts by the door. It seemed like a bad idea to me, but the greeter said that it was OK. I asked her if she could teach him to drive it, but all she did was show him the control that makes it go backward or forward. She didn't even back it out for him, but he enthusiastically climbed aboard. Immediately, he started backing up while looking forward, so I stopped him to show him that he had to look backward as he backed up. He smiled and assured me that he would, but then started right away to back up while looking forward. I stopped him again, went over the rule for backing up, and gently turned his head so he could look backward. I said, "Keep your head like this whenever you back up!" Still smiling, he promised me that he would, but as soon as I took my hand off of his head, he turned his head forward, left the cart in reverse, and hit the throttle. Standing at the first checkout line was a perfectly innocent looking family of four, intent on picking up their bags to carry them out. I yelled, "Look out!" as JH, oblivious to anything but his new ride, backed right into the middle of them. If this was on "America's Funniest Home Videos," they would have played the tape to a bowling alley sound effect. Mom, dad, son, and daughter jumped frantically in four different directions, bags flying, while the checkout clerk looked on in horror as JH crashed into her checkout lane. Now that the family was in his line of vision,

JH realized what he had done and mumbled an apology, as the parents grabbed the kids and the bags and hurried to get a safe distance away. The greeter didn't even take his cart license away, but we agreed to some new rules: he must follow me, with my hand holding the basket, and absolutely no backing up, ever. I revoked his license for his second offense: a fender bender with a clothes rack.

Like a lot of our kids, R came to us with some medical issues, and hers included some complications from a previous abortion. Debbie had to take her to the women's clinic to see an OBGYN a few times. Other girls from the area saw her there, and instead of asking, decided that she must be pregnant, even though she had a tiny waist. She wasn't. But with nothing better to do in this little town but gossip, they decided to guess about who was the baby's father. The busybodies came to the conclusion that, since Debbie was always with her at the doctor, and since she lived with us, that I must be the father! Besides, that would be better gossip than just deciding that she must be pregnant by a boyfriend. R and one of our other girls came home from school one day and told us that some girls had finally asked her about her pregnancy, and if we were covering up that I was the dad. As the father in the house, I always try to be careful, because of nasty-minded gossips like this, and it makes me suspicious of how it is in their family, to think such nasty thoughts.

We took the girls on a mini vacation to Nashville and stayed at a hotel that had an indoor pool. As Tamara was walking to the pool, she spotted a couple of guys. Now, understand, she is pretty enough to turn heads, but this time it was her head that turned for a second look. I'm sure you also understand how important it is for teenage girls to look good and act cool, but it just wasn't happening this time. She walked smack into the glass door by the pool, and not with just a little bump, but with a face-flattening splat. It's a good thing for her that she is the kind of fun person who can laugh at herself. It's a good thing for me, too, since I just told you about it!

We've had lots of kids who were in the band, and JW was one of them. She had told a friend from school about her background, so her friend brought her a phone number that the friend had gotten from a website, done by a man who claimed to want to help abused girls.

JW had some free time during band, and called him a few times from school. Eventually, he drove all the way to Tennessee from Indianapolis, and picked her up during a break in after-school band practice. The school, DCS, JW's friend and her mom, and the police all helped us to find her after she disappeared with him. An obvious tip-off to us, was the fact that on his website, he wanted to see pictures of the girls he was "helping." Now, if someone wants to help you, why does it matter what you look like? It was obvious that he wanted her for prostitution, pornography, sex, or all three. The friend's mom called the phone number that he posted on the web, and it turned out to be his home phone, so she told his wife what he had done. I called the Indianapolis police headquarters and told whoever answered the phone what was going on, in case they knew of him or he took JW home to Indianapolis. The officer on the phone asked me, "And just what do you expect us to do about it?" Since it seemed to me that he should thank me and know what to do, I answered, "Bring me his head on a platter!" Later that night, we had a phone call from JW's mom, saying the JW had gotten away from him and had just called her. When she was picked up, JW had to be taken to a psychiatric hospital, because she was so traumatized that she was suicidal. Parents, the internet dangers are real, and the neediest kids can be the most vulnerable. This girl hadn't seen her dad in many years, and she had always been looking for a man's love.

Most of the guys who target our girls for sex live right here in town, or go to school with our girls. These guys are observant enough to see that our girls can be desperate for attention, and these guys are smooth talkers. They know the compliments and promises that our girls are desperate to hear and believe. Over the years, I hear the same guys, names over and over again, whenever one of our new girls tells us that she has just met a nice guy. We see what's happening; the other girls also tell her about him, but his sweet talk usually fools her. Then it's my job to step in, be the bad guy, and make some enemies. I've learned that dealing with the parents of these boys is usually a waste of time, because the nut doesn't fall very far from the tree. Instead, I deal with the boys personally, through the school, or, most often, through the police and courts. Some boys have been put on probation, and some "adults" have done a little jail time. Our girls say that some guys ignore them, once they find out the girl lives with us, for fear of "catching a charge."

Chapter 14

LET'S NOT SLAP HIM ON THE BACK, LET'S HIT HIM IN THE WALLET

I have titled this book <u>Front Line Observer</u>, because of our experience in residential care. We are in a unique position to observe the battle for the family because we live with the casualties and know their stories. The battle we've observed is between the two sides which are battling for influence over our culture through our families and our kids. On one side are those with the traditional morals, priorities, and values that come from the Judeo-Christian tradition and upon which this nation was founded. This side in the battle is fighting to protect our kids and preserve our families, knowing that whatever destroys our families also destroys our culture. On the other side are those from the atheist, secular, humanistic, and related philosophies which are against absolute morals and teach that right and wrong is situational and ever changing. In order to excuse their lifestyle, they need to remove any influence of Christians and of the church from our society, and to try to intimidate anyone who believes in or lives by traditional values. The other side is willing to destroy our families, kids, and ultimately our culture by redefining the family and marriage until those words and concepts are meaningless. This side even denies that there is a cultural battle, but those of us who are being attacked, or who work with the casualties, know better. The resulting damage done to our kids by this side in the battle is either ignored, redefined as healthy, attributed to the wrong source in order to excuse destructive choices, or is considered acceptable, unimportant collateral damage. I intend to expose this damage that is being done to our kids, and the cause of this damage. I hope to wake up the complacent before it's too late.

Those who want to secularize our society have to remove God, morals, and judgment from public discussion or display. My saying that wrong moral choices have destructive consequences to our families and kids is a judgment that they will attack (if this book gets noticed), but it is nevertheless a fact. They want to say that there is no right or wrong in order to justify themselves. ("They" include most of the entertainment and news media, many colleges, atheists, secularists, many judges, pornographers, humanists, radical feminists, abortionists, and others, such as child abusers and "disappearing dads", who want to excuse their selfish, immature, irresponsible, perverted, violent, and destructive behavior.) I am a simple guy who has made and shared a simple, repeated, and clear observation about the most common trait of the families of our kids, and who feels responsible to share this observation. Ignoring the truth does not make it not true, but it does make trouble. The truth is that the family, which is the foundation of any society, is crumbling. People who try to create a belief system to match or justify their choices ignore this reality and so allow those destructive choices to continue. If you think that it's OK to destroy the family, then you are either choosing not to see that this also destroys our community, or you are willing to destroy it. Check the prisons to see how many of the inmates grew up without dads; it's the same in foster care. Enemies of the family are enemies to our kids, and to the future stability of our society and of our culture.

The observations I present in this book are from our work with kids and families. They are not from my childhood, family, reading, news, my imagination, my agenda, my world view, my education, research, or my faith, but actual, simple observations from a life of living and working with kids. I know that the "politically correct" types like to "kill the messenger" when the message is a warning about the results of a destructive lifestyle choice, so pointing out an observation that leads to the conclusion that certain choices are better than others may get me condemned. Those who want to ignore the reality that immoral sexual choices have a destructive effect on our bodies, relationships, kids, and culture would rather condemn the one who points out the sickness in our society than condemn the ones who are spreading the sickness. Ignoring a sickness does not make it go away, and declaring sickness to be health does not make it so, but instead it spreads the sickness. I believe that the agenda for those who deny this truth is to rationalize their own choices, and so they deny that there is a Creator who is wise and loving and so gives us absolutes that are boundaries designed for our protection.

It is already well known that the sexual, marital, and educational choices made by parents have a major effect on kids. For instance, it is undeniable that being an unmarried, teenage mom greatly increases the chances that the girl and her kids will live in poverty. I have no intention of repeating someone else's work, but I do intend to add to and clarify the body of knowledge that is already out there. Let's understand this fact: Poor choices in the areas of sex, relationships, and marriage result in kids being placed outside the home, and the further consequences that come from separating families. The lists that I have seen of the consequences of teenage pregnancy or of kids born out of wedlock rarely include this truth. I have seen this fact mentioned only in a few publications for those in social work, foster care, or residential care, and I believe that the rest of America needs to be aware of this observation, too. (One agency that has gathered and published some accurate statistics on this subject is the Tennessee Commission on Children and Youth.) I will present a statistic to you that will further define and clarify the most common causes of kids being removed from their family and being placed in foster care, as we have seen it in our kids.

We have known, seen, and worked with healthy families with well adjusted kids in our work with AWANA, our church, at school, and with our relatives and friends. This gives us hope, and healthy families with which to compare the families of our kids. We have also seen and worked with unhealthy families that have troubled and disturbed kids. We don't pretend to know it all, but have observed a lot. We see that having promiscuous sex and having babies from various partners, which is what many think is the answer to their need for love, acceptance, relationships, and intimacy, is actually the cause of much pain. We as a society need to face, admit, and proclaim what we have always instinctively known: that having kids outside of a loving, committed marriage between a man and a woman damages our children.

I didn't begin my work with kids looking for this truth, and I didn't start this book to try to make this point. Over the years, however, this observation has stared me in the face until I couldn't help but notice it, and I can't write a book telling you what I have learned by working with these kids without including the following facts. What is the issue that is most common within the families of the kids who have lived with us? The issue is the fact that in the lives of these kids, there really is no family, at least in the traditional and historically defined sense. There is instead, a poor and unsuccessful counterfeit substitute for a family. This counterfeit has naturally fallen apart, and so Debbie and I have then become the substitute family for the children.

Many in our society have tried to change the definition of family, but these new definitions haven't changed the need that kids have or the consequence of not meeting that need. Defining family as simply people that "care about each other" or who live together or who have sex and make babies together creates counterfeit "families", which in turn make unstable kids and an unstable society. It is clear that kids who do not have the nurturing of a stable, loving family do not make wise choices or thrive and become well-adjusted adults. They don't because some of their needs are not met. These kids, in turn, will not know how to stop this destructive cycle without help, but will repeat the cycle unless they realize the need for help, decide to make different choices than the previous generation, and find the support and help to do so. We must face reality as individuals and as a society. It's this simple: Whatever causes pain to our children and destroys our families is wrong. Period.

Since I do not believe that it is helpful to point out a problem without also suggesting a solution, I have also included ideas for ways to prevent some of the biggest problems we have seen by preventing the biggest cause of the problems that we have seen. You may not like my solutions, but I present them for consideration and challenge anyone who does not like my proposed solutions to come up with some better solutions themselves. Don't just call names, label, complain, accuse, or whine. I have made no attempt to be politically correct, but to merely present our observations clearly. These are not made-up stories or opinions, but factual occurrences and words, and cannot be disputed in themselves. Debate my ideas if you wish, but you can't deny the observations. To dispute the truth of these observations is to deny reality. If you want to debate my conclusions or cures, then go for it, but if you don't have useful, helpful ideas and just want to label me, call names, or throw a fit, then just keep your mouth closed, your pen in your pocket, and your computer off. (Debbie thought it would sound rude if I just told you to shut up.) If you have nothing helpful for the subject, then what you say is invalid and a waste of time. You are part of the problem. I am trying to be part of the solution. If you are offended by recognizing yourself as part of the problem, then face it and help solve it. If you just want to make excuses, then do our kids a favor by staying out of the debate and staying celibate.

Before I tell you my ideas for solutions, I will first describe the common denominators of the families of our kids at the group home, give an example, and then describe a healthy family.

Common Traits of the Families of Our Kids

1. NOT FOLLOWING GOD'S DESIGN FOR A MARRIAGE AND FAMILY. This is the most common trait, and it includes nearly 100% of the families. Since we have lived here at the group home, there have been over two hundred kids placed here with us. Out of all of these kids, only two have come from a traditional, God-designed family. This is the observation that I must emphasize: less than one percent of the families of our kids have been built to the Creator's design. The two exceptions both had the second most common trait, which I will list later. I will also describe God's design later. To get even more specific, it is almost always something about the dad: he was never around, was abusive, left, or was somehow gone and not fulfilling his responsibilities. These following choices and situations are all included in the most common trait:

Mom and dad are not married. Either they were never married, are divorced, are or were living separately, or were married to someone else when mom got pregnant. A very few did marry after one or more of the kids were born.

An unplanned pregnancy, or a pregnancy outside of or before marriage.

Unfaithfulness to each other, whether married or not.

Mom and/or dad have kids with other partners

The father of the child is not known, or the mother won't tell.

Dad, and sometimes even mom, has little, no, or a negative relationship with the child.

Dad is a predator, who seeks out gullible girls, sweet-talks them, gets them pregnant, and goes on to other girls to repeat his pattern.

Dad is irresponsible and selfish. He thinks he can make babies and move on, leaving them for the mom to take care of them.

Note: I'm not saying that everyone who makes such choices will have their kids in foster care; I am saying that almost 100% of kids in foster care come from parents who have made these choices. This first, most common trait is also a cause of some of the other traits, which I list next:

2. Alcohol or drug abuse, by the parent and/or the child. This is the (close) second most common trait, at around 90%, and the two kids who were exceptions to the first trait both had this trait in the family. This trait is already well known and documented, so I won't dedicate much time or space to describe it. In Tennessee, the use of or making of meth in the home by the parents has sadly become a common reason for kids to be removed from the family and from the home.

3. Mothers who were too young to be mature enough to be mothers. Dads were also sometimes too young and almost always too immature. Maybe they have grown older, but not grown up.

4. Parents who were or had been incarcerated, on probation, or had serious legal issues.

The rest of the traits in my list are also common, but are not in any particular order.

5. Poverty and/or government aid.

6. Social isolation. Little or no interaction with anyone outside of the family.

7. Parents were abused as kids, or were in an orphanage, group home, foster home, or detention.

8. Mom has had repeated unhealthy relationships with males, possibly beginning with her dad, and is still looking for a guy to take care of her. This takes priority with her over her own kids.

9. One or both parents have not finished high school. They often don't have their own kids in school, and generally have low educational expectations for themselves and their kids.

10. Abuse between or among each other in the family, including the extended family.

11. Unemployed, or inconsistently employed.

12. Mental health issues or diagnoses.

13. Chaotic, complicated lives. Always in a crisis. They don't recognize that the "freedom" that they think they have actually enslaves them.

14. Other siblings, relatives, or ancestors were or are in an out-of-home placement.

15. Not INVOLVED in church. Maybe they say they attend or belong, but it is sporadic at best.

16. A poor example, dishonest, and a lack of moral character. This has included teaching the kids to shoplift, or to scam the government or social agencies to get money.

17. Unstable, no permanent home, lots of moves, mom lives with her boyfriend or her family.

18. Treat their kids as peers, and not disciplining them. Allow disrespect of parents by kids.

19. Irresponsible, blaming others. They pretend to be helpless victims and admit to little fault.

20. Still putting their own wants over the kid's needs. Still trying to get their own unmet needs met. This kind of woman will choose her abusive boyfriend over her kids, even if she loses them.

21. Parents show lack of self-control; show they need others to control them and/or their kids.

22. Lack of extended family support.

23. Expectation that others will subsidize their destructive choices.

24. Significant difference in age between mom and dad. He is sometimes a father figure to her.

25. Interracial relationships. (This is not listed to condemn this choice, but I would be dishonest not to include it, since we have had a higher percentage of kids from interracial relationships than we see in the general population. This was particularly obvious during our time in Maryland.)

26. The kids have already tried living with other relatives. Mom has often sabotaged this or the chance for the kids to be adopted by others.

27. Mom and dad cannot trust or depend upon each other. They often blame each other.

28. Idle lives. Life consists of talking on the phone, gossip, TV, sex and making babies, and complaining that the government does not take better care of them, instead of working.

29. The priority is not the children or the marriage. This is the kind of parent who will not find a way to visit the child, take the child for a weekend or holiday, or work to get the child back home.

30. She and/or he keep making babies, even though they can't care for, handle, afford, or keep the kids the already have.

31. Confusion between the roles of parents and children, or even reversals of these natural roles.

It may be helpful if I describe a common situation. (This is an example, not a particular family.) Mom was pregnant at 15. He was a little older. Both used drugs. They never married, and in spite of his promises, he left. They kept in touch for awhile, but now the only time she knows where he lives is when he's in jail. She didn't finish school. Both had kids by other people. Mom eventually married, but it didn't last. Mom moved in and out with boyfriends and relatives. One of her boyfriends abused her daughter, but she blames the daughter. The daughter has no respect for mom and no bond with dad. She starts to skip school, run away, and gets in a little legal trouble. The judge sees that mom can't protect or supervise her and commits her to state custody. Then we get a call from the foster care workers, asking if she can live here.

Now I will define a family. You may call it the natural family, the traditional family, the historic family, the ideal family, or the nuclear family. I will call it the God-designed family.

1. Mom and dad are married, forever, and only once, unless widowed. One man and one woman.

2. There was no living together before marriage, and no kids before marriage.

3. There is one mom, one dad, and all of the kids belong to both mom and dad. Unless one parent has died and the surviving parent has remarried, there are no half or step siblings.

4. The family has strong sexual morals. Both parents are faithful to each other. There is no incest.

5. There is no divorce, unless one parent has already ruined the design by being unfaithful, abusive, or has abandoned the family. Divorce is an option only if there is unfaithfulness, or to protect

someone from abuse. This couple does not enter marriage with divorce as an option.

6. The family lives together. The kids stay until grown, and the parents "till death do us part."

7. Dad meets mom's needs and "loves her as Christ loved the church."

8. Adopting kids is a great option, and is clearly part of the Designer's plan.

There are undeniable advantages to kids who have parents who love and are committed to each other and to the kids. The most well-adjusted kids are the ones who live with both mom and dad and have the confidence that comes from being certain that mom and dad love them and love each other unconditionally, and that mom and dad will always remain together.

It is clear to all of us in this kind of work that we need to encourage everyone to be married before they have kids, and that we need to discourage unwed people, especially teens, from having kids. If it's not clear to you yet, go back and read the rest of this book. We must require our men to be dependable, so women won't have to depend upon the government. The one who is primarily responsible for supporting an unwed mom and her kids is the same as if she is married: the one who got her pregnant! The pervert who got her pregnant needs to experience the "you play, you pay" principle. After him, her support can come from his or her family, followed by the church or charities, and finally from the taxpayers, but only as a last resort safety net. On the front line of this particular part of the battle are the family and the church. (This is too important to leave just to the government.) They need to be the teachers, the support system, the example, and the conscience. The suggestions I am about to make, however, are for the next line of defense against those whose perverted immorality hurts our kids. This line of defense is our government, as a representative for and agent of society as a whole. So many unwed moms expect the government to pay for everything (including foster care), and so many unwed dads get out of their responsibility. We need to raise the stakes for these dads. So as incentives to behaving responsibly, I make these following suggestions. There will be no generalities or hand-wringing whining for the government to come up with ideas. Our observations are facts, and so they are not open to debate, but you may debate my suggestions. Here they are:

1. No income tax deduction or earned income credit for a child unless the parents were and are married to each other, or were married until widowed. A related option is to give the earned income credit money in a pre-paid card, which is useable only to purchase what kids need. EIC is to help working families to provide for the children. I have seen it wasted on things such as jewelry or spending cash for a father who was too irresponsible to pay for the needs of a child.

2. Mom must identify dad. Mandatory DNA tests if there is a dispute over who is the father, and the cost for the test covered by the mom and/or dad. (He pays if the mom is a child.)

3. Mandatory child support will be collected from any dad not married to the baby's mom, retroactive to pregnancy. The costs begin before the baby is born.

4. Mandatory sexually transmitted disease (STD) tests for all (mom, dad, and the baby if mom or dad tests positive) if an unmarried woman or girl is pregnant. There can be no privacy rules or laws regarding STDs for anyone having sex outside of marriage. In this case, health concerns trump privacy concerns. STDs are not spread by those who follow the Creator's design.

5. A nationwide STD registry, available to all, and a felony to have sex without full, prior disclosure of all STDs. STDs are spread by those who don't follow the Creator's design for sex.

6. No AFDC or other assistance from taxpayers unless mom and dad are married. The exception to this would be government help for mom to get child support from an absent dad.

7. After the first baby, some kind of birth control (for both mom and dad), that doesn't require a daily pill or thinking responsibly before sex. Multiple offenders get permanent surgery.

8. No free or subsidized government child care or housing. She may stay if she is already in government housing, but doesn't get her rent lowered just because she had a baby, and she may get a bigger unit only if she is able to pay more for it. We can't reward bad behavior.

9. Subsidized food and medical care only for the baby, any prenatal needs, and delivery. This is needed only if dad refuses to pay, and in such a case must be repaid to the government through a garnishment of any source of his present or future income, or by property confiscation.

10. No public funds or support of any kind for abortion. (This includes no taxpayer funding for Planned Parenthood.) Abortion is an extreme form of child abuse, and is physically and psychologically dangerous for the mother. Abortion dehumanizes babies and gives our kids the dangerous messages that children have no value, and that it is OK to use violence on innocent victims. The availability of abortion encourages irresponsible sex by providing an after-the-fact birth control method for those who want to avoid the inconvenience of the consequences for their choices by murdering their baby. There is no "safe" abortion, and it's not a "reproductive rights" or "women's health" issue. Abortion is murder! Choose adoption instead! A dad may never force a mom to have an abortion, and may not refuse to pay child support because she refuses to kill their baby for his convenience.

11. Encourage adoption by raising subsidies to the actual cost of care. This cost can come from garnishing the dad's paycheck or other income, as is done for child support payments.

12. A national deadbeat dad list, available to anyone, so he can't hide his selfishness.

13. A national "family tree" registry, open to anyone who has a need to see if a partner or potential partner (or any mom or dad) already have kids or have other kids from another partner. A woman should know if the guy who wants date her, marry her, or have sex with her already has

kids. If he does, she needs to insist on knowing why he is asking for a relationship, marriage, or sex from someone other than the mother of his kids, and whether or not he is taking care of his kids. This registry could also be useful for making sure that a woman is aware that her unfaithful husband has gotten someone pregnant, or for child support collection and enforcement.

14. Vigorously enforce rape laws. Strengthen them to include a provision that says if the victim gets pregnant and wants to keep the baby, then she is eligible to get child support from the rapist if she wants it. If she chooses to give the baby up for adoption, he gets no say in the matter and can be required to pay all prenatal or adoption expenses. Felons have to pay up, too!

15. Both mom and dad are required to contribute to an educational fund and medical expense fund for the child, just as if they would if they were married and saving money together.

16. Dad cannot qualify for any college scholarship, unless he is paying his fair share of expenses for the child. He needs to get a job or join the military so he can pay child support.

17. Mandatory adoption counseling, to be paid for by the father. If mom chooses to have someone adopt the baby, dad can still be held responsible for the costs of pregnancy and delivery.

18. Drinking alcohol or doing drugs while pregnant should be defined as a form of child abuse. If mom abuses her baby this way, she may be required to go into treatment, and she will be required to pay the cost of any treatment or follow-up needed for her and/or the baby.

19. Limit and enforce access to perverted music, internet, movies, TV,(especially videos), etc. for kids. MTV, BET, or similar video channels always need to be optional, extra-cost channels in all cable or satellite systems. An R-rated movie, or any movie that shows extra-marital sex without realistic consequences requires the child to be with a parent, not just any adult. Rentals or sales of such movies can be to adults only. Maybe we can have a new "P" rating (for Perverted)

movies or TV. Any music that glorifies, brags about, or encourages sex outside of marriage is rated R, P, or X, and is banned from any free radio station. Music or music videos which include this kind of music, dancing, or message are sold only to adults.

20. If he does not pay enough child support, confiscate his money, assets, or possessions. These may be given to the mom or kids, or sold to cover child support payments. Declaring bankruptcy cannot be an excuse for not paying child support. Child support will still be expected.

21. If he marries someone else later, he must first give his new wife-to-be a full disclosure of all of his kids, who is the mother of his kids, and how much child support he pays or owes.

22. If he does not take care of his financial responsibilities for the child, he is put on Pervert Probation, carry an IPID (Irresponsible Pervert ID) card at all times, and report to a Pervert Probation officer as ordered. He must show his IPID to anyone he asks for a date (and to her parents, if she is a child), anyone he marries, or to his partner before any sexual activity.

23. Mom and dad must both post a bond, in order to cover expenses in case anyone else becomes responsible to care for the child. If unused, this bond can be used for the child's college.

24. The child is covered by the father's medical and life insurance, and Social Security.

25. If mom or dad is married to someone else, the spouse can divorce them for unfaithfulness and get everything. This includes the children, if they wish, and full child support.

26. No statute of limitations for collecting child support. Your kids can sue for it, too.

27. No public or subsidized housing if living together unmarried. No overnight "visits."

28. No credit will be given unless child support and bond are consistently paid on time.

29. At retirement, any unpaid child support, child expenses, or bond comes out of IRA or SS before dad collects any money. This also goes for any income tax refunds, inheritance, bonds, stock dividend, sales of property, lottery winnings, lawsuit settlements, or any other money source. An adult child can sue a deadbeat dad anytime, and can be named co-owner of his business.

30. If the government cares for or pays to care for your child, (such as for foster care, residential or psychiatric treatment), you are on birth control until you get your child back and have paid the expenses. Maybe someone can invent a modern day chastity belt for you instead.

31. Rapists can be castrated and/or branded. How about inventing a "crotch stock"? It could be used on him in prison. Or maybe invent some "chastity pants" for rapists to wear.

32. If he does not get a job, he can be assigned a government job or be drafted into the military so he can pay child the support and bond.

33. Another option if he won't work, is to be placed on an IPWC (Irresponsible Pervert Work Crew), to pay his responsibilities. There can even be an IPWC work camp, where his work pays for his room, board, and uniform, and then goes to pay off any responsibilities for the child.

34. A maternity leave, with a guarantee to be able to return her job, could be a perk for married moms only.

35. Reward married parents or those who accomplish marriage milestones (10 years, 20 years, etc.) with higher tax credits or deductions (especially if one stays home to care for kids). Be fair to families by getting rid of any marriage penalty in the income tax system.

36. Mom and dad must donate money and/or time to IPR, (Irresponsible Pervert Reduction) programs. Any repeat offender or public figure or celebrity, such as entertainers, sports figures, or

politicians must donate A LOT, according to their wealth, power and/or fame or potential influence over others. Entertainers involved in an IPR program must donate time to making music, movies or videos which show realistic consequences to sex or having babies outside of marriage, and must strongly encourage kids not to follow their immature, selfish examples. Any commercial projects in which they are involved must give the same message.

37. The enforcement costs of these ideas are charged to dad and mom (unless she is a rape victim). Enforcement and collection of child support crosses state and international borders.

38. If alcohol was involved in the incident by which an unwed mom became pregnant, the person that used alcohol may no longer go to bars or have, buy, sell, serve, or drink alcohol.

39. If he is an illegal alien, confiscate his property and deport him, unless he marries her.

40. Mom or dad may not work as a teacher, or any other job where they would be the authority, example, law enforcer, or protector for kids until they get married, or set a date for it.

41. We must all face reality about condoms. Condoms give a false sense of security and encourage risky behavior. We need to be teaching and expecting strong morals and wise choices instead of giving permission to act irresponsibly. Passing out condoms to kids encourages the foolish, destructive fantasies that man has invented a way to avoid natural consequences for behavior, and that there is no need to develop or exercise self control. Maybe manufactures and distributors of condoms who don't warn of ineffectiveness should be held liable in case of pregnancies or STDs. There should be no taxpayer funding of condom distribution or of organizations that distribute condoms to kids, especially to any abortionists such as Planned Parenthood who profit from selling abortions to those for whom the condoms have failed.

42. Whoever is caring for the child gets a pre-paid expense card, to use for the child's expenses. This card is purchased by the mom and/or dad with child support money.

43. "Safe sex" is not just avoiding STDs or unwanted pregnancy. We must teach the cost and consequences of out-of wedlock babies. We must instill character strength and discernment.

44. If you make a baby outside of marriage, you can't be appointed to be a judge or be elected to public office until after you are married. Your poor example would be as much of a danger for our society as appointing or electing a convicted felon, and so will be treated the same.

The following additional suggestions are for a situation in which one of the unmarried parents is a child and the other is an adult, or if both of the parents are children:

45. Ignorance of his/her age is no excuse, and a child can't seduce or control an adult.

46. The child will be required to complete high school; child care to be paid by the adult.

47. Bill expenses to his parents if he is a minor and in school or a juvenile facility, and so can't earn enough. He should take over financial responsibility as soon as possible.

48. Full immunity for the parents of a child who has been raped or abused by an adult, for anything the parents do to the adult, short of killing them or inflicting a permanent injury.

49. There can be a marriage if the child and the child's parents desire it, and the court OKs it. If the adult refuses marriage, then the child still gets full rights, financial or otherwise, just as if married. If the child or parents don't want a marriage, the child still gets the same financial rights.

50. Strengthen and enforce underage drinking laws. If the child is drinking or drugged, then they cannot consent to sex, either with an adult or another child, and so it is rape.

51. The adult is banned from anywhere the child usually goes, any school or anywhere where there are kids' activities or where kids congregate. This includes the mall.

52. The parent or court can ban the adult from any kind of communication with the child.

53. Prosecute! No "slap on the back" sentences! This includes female teachers.

54. The child and parents of the child need to sue the adult in civil court for all expenses.

Note: Where appropriate, some of these suggestions will have exceptions for moms who are widows or rape victims. In cases of rape, the victim needs to cooperate (with reasonable expectations) to help identify and prosecute the rapist. Most rapists are known to the victims.

Some of these suggestions will cost money, but the cost will be less than the cost to society for all of these fatherless babies. We must recognize the cost of perversion, and that sexual "freedom" isn't free of consequences or cost. You may think I am picking on the dads, but most of the time the moms and their families are already taking care of the baby, and I want the dads to be equally responsible. Both parties need to know that all of us are expected to show some self control, or someone else must control us. These suggestions will take awhile to work; maybe three generations. This problem of fatherless babies didn't happen overnight and there is no quick cure. Long term change will be one dad, one child, and one family at a time. I hope these suggestions are useful to help solve the problem, or are at least useful to begin a national discussion about how to solve the problem. If you have a better idea, then let's hear it; if you don't have any of your own ideas, then you don't get to criticize. To show you that I'm serious about this problem, I would like to volunteer my own town to try out some of these ideas. I even know a couple of guys on whom we can test these ideas, and I'm ready to begin.

Perversion causes pain. Perverts must be held accountable for the consequences of their perversion. If it's illegal to be married to more than one woman, then why should it be OK to have lots of "baby mamas"? We can't continue to allow those who make babies, when they know that they can't afford or handle them, to continue to expect the rest of us to pay the bills. Dads: if we can't make you spend time with your kids, we can make you spend your money on them. If you refuse to act responsibly, then you must pay someone else to care for your responsibilities. The poverty in which these kids and moms live is avoidable, by making wise choices, and its time for enough of us to get angry about it. Righteous anger, properly channeled, can produce good results. We must be passionate about protecting our kids. The casualty count of our kids in the battle for the family is way too high. Perversion is not to be accepted, tolerated, "understood," or "treated," but it is to be recognized, rejected, prevented, and punished.

Chapter 15

PARENTS, DON'T TRY THIS AT HOME!

If there is one subject about which we have learned during our years of residential work, it is the subject of what the parents and kids have done or not done, that resulted in the kids being placed in residential care. We can tell you the steps that were taken by the families that resulted in the family coming apart temporarily or permanently. I talked about this subject in the chapter titled "The Difference", and I will now approach it briefly again, from a different direction.

Here are six simple steps to take if you want to have your kids removed from your care:
(Remember, the root word of ignorant is "ignore!")

1. Ignore God's instructions.

Since these instructions are in the Bible, then it would be too dangerous to read. The Bible might give you wisdom or even worse: lead to a change in your way of thinking or behavior. It could cause you to be humble, loving, and unselfish.

Never get involved In a Bible-teaching church. The fact that kids who are heavily involved in a good church almost never end up in foster care is just a coincidence.

Just because God created you, knows the future, and loves you enough to make the ultimate sacrifice for you doesn't mean that He knows more than you.

You can be your own god, so you can decide what's right or wrong, and when.

That stuff about teaching your kids? That's the school's job! You're busy!

What about that honoring your husband or wife stuff? They need to honor you!

That stuff about loving others as much as yourself? Any politically correct person can tell you that the Bible is full of dangerous philosophy like this!

Ignore other books by Christian authors, too. Anybody who teaches that you need to put your family above your job, social life, habits, and hobbies must be a kook!

2. Ignore common sense, time-proven wisdom, experience, the natural order, and reality.

Ignore this book. Don't read the other chapters. I don't know anything about kids who come into foster care, and you know more than anyone else, anyway.

Make sure you ignore your parents. They don't know anything about kids or you.

Ignore the natural fact that it takes a man and a woman to make a baby. The guy's job is done after his sperm has penetrated the egg. The baby in her is just hers.

Ignore the fact that most guys in jail had little or no relationship with their dads.

Ignore the facts that kids who live with only one parent are much more likely to do poorly in school, have emotional problems, and live in poverty. That's other folks. Kids are here to meet the needs of their parents, not the other way around.

Don't discipline your kids. Get angry at anyone else who disciplines them.

3. Ignore morals, traditional values, and laws.

It doesn't matter if you have committed to each other by getting married and staying together. The insecurity will just make your kids grow up stronger.

It's your body! It doesn't matter how many people you have sex with, or how many babies you have, as long as the government will pay for your medical bills, day care, rent, and food. You pay taxes!

It's OK if all your babies are by different guys, and he has other "baby mommas." Your kids won't get confused or be treated any differently. You neglect them all!

It's OK; you need your drugs and alcohol more than your kids need you.

Your money is for cigarettes and the casino; if any is left you can use it for bills.

4. Ignore your responsibilities.   (It's not your fault!)

After all, you are the center of the universe and your wants come first.

Guys: She knew what she was doing when she got pregnant! Don't let her trap you like that! Someone else can provide for your kids. You need to buy drugs!

Your kids can get themselves up and go to school. You need your sleep.

Never know what your kids are doing, so you can tell the judge it's not your fault.

Ignore any notes from school or invitations to meetings. They don't like your kid.

The teachers can show them how to do their homework. It's not your grade!

Set an example? That's what the TV is for! Or maybe her older sister. Let other parents set your standard for what you will allow your kid to wear or do. That way, the worst parent in the community can set the standard for everyone.

5. Ignore your kids.

Someone else will watch them, teach them, nurture them, provide for them, protect them, and set an example for them. What about your parents? They're not busy and they did such a good job with you! Besides, the school, day care, church, courts, and government are supposed to do all of that stuff. You need all of your attention for you, anyway. Who's going to meet your attention needs?

It's OK if you hardly ever spend time with your kids, as long at its "quality time."

They have a TV and computer, anyway. MTV raised you and you turned out OK!

He can learn to be a responsible man without his dad setting an example. Maybe his coach or his gang or his probation officer can do that. You have another family.

She can learn what it's like to have a man love her without her dad's love. She'll know how to recognize and get real love. After all, look how well her mom did!

You need to watch your soap operas, be at the bar with your friends, find your next fix, or look for a new boyfriend or girlfriend. The job takes all your free time.

Your new boyfriend doesn't like it when your kids are around. He needs his sex.

6.   Ignore the signs.

Ignore the police, school counselor, or the kid's psychiatrist or probation officer.

Ignore the kid's cries for attention or acting out. You don't want to spoil him.

Finally, if the court won't take the kids off your hands, then just volunteer to give them up. You have more important things to do! They're interrupting your lifestyle! If you want kids, you can make more or move in with someone who has some.

Obviously, unless you started reading this book with this chapter, you know that these are the steps we DON'T want you to take. Keep your kids! We have enough, thank you. If you choose to take these steps, you are choosing to destroy your family. Since the families are the building blocks of society, your selfishness and immaturity hurt the rest of us, too. You need to have an operation or at least keep your pants on so you won't do this to any more of our kids!

Chapter 16

DADS, I'M TALKING TO YOU

Her name was Suzy. She was a blonde-haired Cocker Spaniel mix.. She was already here at the group home when we came in 1987, but we adopted her as ours, and she was with us for over ten years. She was pretty, smart, full of joy, and great with the kids. But she wasn't great with her puppies. One November, she had a litter of eight puppies. She seemed to have no idea what was going on, because as she was delivering, she was walking around the yard. She would just drop a puppy on the ground and move on. When I saw what she was doing, I called her name, and as always, she came running happily up to me. We took her inside and put her in a box lined with a blanket, where she had the last couple of puppies. Meanwhile, everyone was looking around the yard until we were sure that we had found all eight of the puppies. Once they were all in the box, her instinct kicked in and she began to lick them and feed them. After that, she did pretty well, and even nursed a stray kitten along with the puppies. She sometimes acted like she would rather be with us than her puppies, and we would have to put her back into her box to feed them. She also acted jealous of the puppies when we would give them attention. Don't worry, the puppies got plenty of love here, and they were all eagerly taken home by the families of our kids. However, we decided to have her "fixed" after this, and so that was her only litter.

Too many of you guys act like Suzy; making babies and acting like they aren't even there, or dropping them off at various places like Suzy was doing in the yard. She didn't know better, but you do! Your kids need you like her puppies needed her, but you act like what you want is more important than what your kids need. If you act like Suzy did, you aren't ready to be a dad. If you aren't ready for the responsibilities of fatherhood, then you need to keep your pants on. What solved the problem in Suzy's situation was having someone else care for the puppies, and then having surgery to make sure she couldn't have any more. We've taken care of a lot of your kids, and maybe the best thing to do is for you to have surgery so you can't have any more, either.

Now, I know that this applies to some moms, too, and I'm not a man-hating radical feminist dupe. What I am is a man that wants other men to act like men, not selfish little boys. We know lots of guys who are good dads, but we also know too many who have ignored their responsibility to be a parent or who have delegated their responsibility to someone else.

If I were an observer in the army, who was assigned to the front lines of a battle, I would be in derelict of duty if I didn't report exactly what I saw, as soon as possible. If I could spot and recognize the deceptions of an enemy sneak attack, I would save lives by reporting it. It would be stupid for my superiors to get angry with me for reporting what I saw, and to ignore my warnings. I would expect my observations to be taken seriously and acted upon. I would also expect the enemy to want to neutralize me by eliminating me or deceiving the others into believing that I'm wrong. Like in a battle, you are either with us or against us, and in this battle for our kids you are either part of the solution or part of the problem.

If I were your doctor, and I told you that your diet choices were making you unhealthy, it wouldn't be "hate speech" or promoting violence toward the overweight. It would be a sign of wisdom, experience, and caring about you. We don't welcome viruses into our bodies for fear of judging or offending the virus or not being "inclusive" or "tolerant." We work to prevent pain and destruction by keeping the destructive virus out. It only makes sense to reject or "exclude" whatever is destroying us. Likewise, I'm not "mean spirited" or promoting violence toward the perverted, but sharing observations of what works with kids and families, and what destroys them.

There are some who will get angry because I have pointed out that the most common reasons for kids to be in foster care are moral reasons, but the one who points out the problem isn't the problem. The doctor who tells you that you have a disease didn't give you the disease. If he tells you to stop doing something that is destroying you, then you would be wise to change your habits. The first steps to a cure are acknowledging that you are sick and identifying the cause. Our motivation is love, not hate. We don't hate unwed moms or dads, and we certainly don't hate their kids. (We love Tamara and our granddaughter, Alydia!) Part of our philosophy in residential ministry is that we love you just like you are, but we love you too much to let you stay that way. It has become fashionable for the "politically correct" to try to attach negative labels, such as "intolerant," to anyone who speaks of morals or of the consequences of immoral sexual choices. The people who actually are intolerant are the hypocritical politically correct types who attempt to censor values or any message that doesn't agree with their closed-minded opinions, but I will not be censored. Those of us with morals get to speak too, and we will not be intimidated. We have seen the results of the toleration of men who abandon their kids. Someone needs to say this, so I will: Morally correct works better for our kids than politically correct!

I have never seen a boy who received too much positive attention from his dad go into foster care. I've never seen a girl who was "over protected" by her parents go into foster care. I've never seen a mother who let herself by used by multiple men or searched for happiness in multiple partners/husbands who was happy, content, or joyful. I've never seen any of our girls who had the same poor taste in boys as their mom find the intimacy, respect, security, fulfillment, commitment, and love for which they are searching. I have seen the cycle continue, though, due to a girl insisting on looking for love in the wrong place, and repeating her own or her mom's misguided choices. Giving sex outside of marriage or to multiple partners does not buy love. Repeating the same mistake does not accomplish a better result. It buys pain for the girl and for the next generation. The true "love child" is a baby who is born into a loving, committed marriage, and not the child of an unwed mom and dad with so little self-control and so much selfishness that they have an affair. This is true if you are a homeless junkie, an NBA player, or a senator from the royal family of Massachusetts. Until we require our guys to be men, in other words responsible, respectful, accountable, and unselfish, we can expect more pain for our kids and more damage to our society.

The good news is that there is a time-honored prevention for the pain and damage suffered by so many of our kids. It's called a loving marriage. Let's face the facts, practice the prevention, and deal firmly with those who choose to be the cause of pain for our kids. Education alone isn't enough for humans to alter their behavior; humans need motivation, too. I have seen the problem often described as unwed mothers, but it is even more of a problem of unwed fathers. At least the mothers often keep the child; the "fathers" often leave the care of the baby solely to the mother. This kind of guy is still a boy, no matter how many years he has lived or how many girls he has gotten pregnant, because he's irresponsible.

It's time for dads to step up and be men. It's time for all of us to be honest. It's time to stop calling behavior that causes pain and the destruction of families "alternative lifestyles". It's time to stop overlooking, excusing, and subsidizing irresponsible, promiscuous, destructive behavior. We already have way too many kids of the current generation who haven't ever seen or been nurtured in a family that works, and these kids are making babies themselves, already. It's time to get out of this cycle. It's time to show our sons how to be good dads. It's time to set a better example and expect better behavior. It's time to condemn destructive behavior and hold responsible those who cause pain to our children. It's time to meet the needs of our kids. It's time to recognize our errors and repent. It's time to stop treating women who make a choice to be unwed mothers as victims. Parents, it's time for us to stop enabling our daughters by caring for their babies while our daughters go out to play. It's time to stop enabling our sons by insulating them from the consequences of their choices. It's time to recognize the fact that what one of us does affects the rest of us. It's time to stop treating perversion as normal or acceptable. It's time to stop confusing perversion with progress. It's time to elevate and honor marriage. It's time to pass the Marriage Protection Amendment. It's time to recognize that having kids comes with responsibility. It's time to stop portraying dads on TV as clueless morons. It's time for unwed dads to stop behaving like the clueless morons we see on TV. It's time to stop mocking those who (like Dan Quayle) are brave enough to speak the truth. It's time to stop being so worried about not "judging" others or being called "insensitive" that we allow those who cause pain to our kids to continue inflicting pain. It's time to be sensitive to our kids, instead. It's time to recognize the value of a marriage and the value of our children. It's time to expose the lies and to stop using dishonest terms like "reproductive rights" to refer to choices or lifestyles that damage or destroy our kids. It's time to realize that morals and character matter. It's time to insist on the inclusion of morals, common sense, and a conscience in our "inclusive" society. It's time to confront those who make casualties of our kids. This includes the "men" who unashamedly make babies and abandon them, but it also includes anyone who tries to justify this kind of behavior by pretending that there are no moral absolutes, or that anyone has a "right" to behave in such a way that hurts our kids. It's time to reject the idea of re-defining marriage and family in order to justify destructive or unnatural lifestyles, and to rebuild the boundaries that protect our kids and families from being the casualties in the culture war. It's time to stand up for our kids and for the self evident truth that a woman cannot be or replace a dad, and a man cannot be or replace a mom. It's time for those who care about kids to step up and enlist in the battle to protect our kids. It's time to stop being intimidated by the name calling and lies of those who hate the truth. Debbie and I have seen firsthand and have lived with the results of what America has tolerated and accepted, and now is threatening to dominate and destroy us, and I refuse to just let this happen.

My main points seem obvious to those of us on the front line, and so they seem like they should not need to be said, but just as obviously, they must be said. Kind of like some of the obvious things that you think you should never have to tell your kids, but you discover that you must, anyway. Like a caring parent who wants to keep a child from pain and self-destructive choices, I want to keep pain and self-destructive choices out of our families. I hope to accomplish this by sharing what we have learned, and by including our observations in the national conversation. The three main points that our kids need for you to remember are:

1. The evidence I see demonstrates that most common reason that kids are in foster care is that the parents have not followed God's

design or instructions for a family. This is the common thread that unites nearly all of the kids in residential care here at the group home.

2   Unwed motherhood is a big problem; unwed fatherhood is an even bigger problem.

Dad not fulfilling his responsibility is a factor in nearly 100 percent of families who have had their children taken away from them and placed with us. If every dad would fulfill his responsibility toward his wife and kids, there would be very few kids in foster care.

3.   Kids need to be raised by both a mom and a dad. Married parents are the most effective parents. When dad is gone, his kids are the casualties.

EACH OF OUR KIDS HAS A STORY

Choosing which stories to tell has been one of the most difficult tasks that I have attempted while writing this book. Each child and family we have encountered has multiple layers of stories, and so I've attempted to choose a variety. Some are about what has happened here, and some are about what happened at home. I hope that some have made you smile, some have made you angry, and that many have made you think. Some are unique, and some represent the experience of many of our kids. Each is as accurate as we can remember. Here are a few more stories. If my stories leave you wanting more, then I may have to write another book.

Altogether, mom had thirteen kids, by various men. At one time or another, and in various states, each of her kids has been in state custody. I haven't even attempted to add up the monetary cost to the taxpayers of caring for her kids, and I know of no way to add up the cost to our society of the choices that this woman continued to make. It didn't matter to her, though, because as long as she had at least one child with her, she could still draw her government check. This is what her kids have told us about her. In addition to her check, she has attempted numerous other scams in order to cheat the government out of money, and has involved her kids in some of these scams. Three of her sons were with us, at various times, but the only family member who called the boys with any regularity was an older sister. Mom was too busy with her scams, and at times it was too risky (for her) for the boys to even know how to contact her.

One of our rules, here, is that parents must be sober in order to pick up their kids for a few hours or a weekend together. Parents have embarrassed or disappointed the kids by showing up for a visit drunk or high. Sometimes, the parents get drunk and forget. Other times, the parents are drunk when they bring the kids back to us. The danger of driving their kids while drunk, or losing the privilege of taking their kids with them somewhere, is less important than getting a buzz, and the kids can see this as well as we see it. Of course, we also then must deal with the issue of whether or not the child is also stoned or has been drinking with mom or dad. One mom, who was supposed to have her son for the day, dropped him off at his girlfriend's house, and gave him money to buy marijuana. Another mom wrapped bottles of hard liquor inside of rolled-up shirts to give to her daughter for her birthday present. Dads promise to come and see their kids, but there isn't any gas money left after he uses it to buy his crack cocaine. Don't try to tell us that alcohol or drug abuse is a victimless crime; the victims live here with us.

Promiscuity is one of the most common traits of girls who have either been sexually abused, ignored by their dads, or who have had a poor moral example from their mom. This is one of the reasons that the cycle continues, because promiscuity leads to more fatherless babies. Sexual immorality is also damaging, and in some cases slowly killing our kids, especially our girls. Dozens of our girls have had an STD. Some had the disease before they moved in here, and some have contacted an STD after they were gone, in spite of STD prevention both here and at school. Education is clearly a critical part of the response to the STD epidemic, but good information alone will not change the behavior habits of our kids. (If you believe that information by itself will lead to good habits, you haven't tried to teach a teenager to drive.) Our girls are promiscuous for a reason; they are trying to meet a need. Bodies have developed, but character, wisdom, insight, foresight, self respect, and strength haven't developed, so they don't recognize the need that they are trying to meet and aren't mature enough to be able to identify a healthy way to meet the need. This need that I'm talking about is the need for the love, acceptance, and attention that our girls didn't get from their dad. They need to be noticed, wanted, cherished, and treasured, but they believe the myth that sex by itself satisfies this need. The answer isn't to give up on the next generation and pass out condoms, just so that we can pretend we are doing something about the epidemic. The answer is to be sure that our daughters have their needs met, but in a physically, morally, and psychologically healthy way. As much as movies and music have taught our girls to dress and act like prostitutes, our girls would be much less likely to follow the perverted messages and examples of so many of the current "artists" if dad would give them the love they need, and mom would give them the example they need.

This isn't a story about one girl; it's the story of many of our girls. Debbie has taken them to the clinic to have the warts that come with the HPV virus frozen or chemically burned off. She has taken them for their HIV screening every six months, if we know that they've been exposed to it. We have had girls who have an "Oh, well!" attitude and knowingly continue to spread the STD to others, and we have had other girls who worry about dying from cervical cancer someday. Parents, if you love your kids, then be sure that your daughters have their need for love met in the home, and that your sons see that the way to be a real man is to treat women with the respect due to a priceless treasure.

BP would watch for opportunities at school to steal money from anyone who was careless, or beg money from anyone who was generous. She learned this from her mom, along with how to respond with aggression or hysterics whenever she was caught. Even though her mom didn't visit and almost never called during BP's 17-month stay here, BP was loyal to her mom and tried to imitate her. One of BP's excuses for hoarding the money that she had begged from others was that her mom needed it. One of her attempts to hide stolen money was to dig a small hole in the wall above the desk in her bedroom, and put the money into the hole. She didn't realize that the money would fall all the way down to the floor, so she dug another hole in the wall. The hole above the desk was hidden behind a photo, but we found the hole that she had dug near the floor, and the money that was in it. BP was furious that we actually gave the money back to the child at school from whom she had stolen it, reasoning that once it was in BP's possession, that it belonged to her.

When it came to her neglectful mom, however, she was a generous little girl. Some men from our church had given us some cash, which was to be used by the girls to buy Christmas gifts for each other. The girls drew names in order to choose which of the other girls for whom they would buy a gift., but instead of buying for the girl whose name she drew, BP spent all of her money on some expensive shoes for her mom. When we reminded her that the money was for a gift for another one of our girls, who wouldn't be getting a gift, now BP's answer was, "But I know my mom needs shoes!" At Christmas, mom didn't have a gift for BP, but BP reasoned that mom must not have any money. The truth is that mom used her money on herself, because she had never grown out of the "all about me" stage enough to be a parent. A child, in the thoughts of someone like this, is just another person to manipulate for their own agenda. BP was moved around a lot, including with relatives who tried to help, but never went back with her mom, because mom would never do what it would take to get her back.

Chris and Dave were two of the boys in our house in the Dominican Republic. Dave had a girlfriend, Tracy, who lived at the girls' house nearby. Tracy was cute, and Chris had a crush on her, but had kept it secret. Tracy was about to return home to her mom in the USA, and according to the school tradition, visited all of the houses at the boarding school on her last night so that she could say good-bye to everyone. Chris decided that this was the time to tell Tracy that he had always had a crush on her. As they talked out in the yard, Chris told her how he loved her, but had never said anything until then because of Dave. He wanted to tell her now, because they would never see each other again. She was going to be leaving for the airport early the next morning, before school, and they lived in different states. After Tracy left, Chris told all of us what he had said to her. Dave told him that it was OK and that the boys would still be friends, because Tracy would be gone.

Later that night, however, Tracy's mom called the school administrator to say that she had decided that she wasn't ready for Tracy to return home, and not to put Tracy on the airplane home! We knew nothing about this at our house, though, until I drove the boys to school the next morning. There was Tracy, sitting on the front porch of the school, waiting to go to class! Both boys looked at me; Dave with a look of surprise, and Chris with that wide-eyed "deer in the headlights" look of absolute terror. Dave asked, "What's Tracy doing still here?" but Chris could only mumble a weak, "Oh no!", and sink down into the seat of the van. Tracy, of course, must have been angry and humiliated already, and now also had an awkward social situation to navigate. I was proud of her, though, as she smiled sweetly and said "Hi" to both boys. She kept doing well at school, as far as I know, but I imagine that she had a hard time rebuilding any trust in her mom.

RB was one of the boys who already lived here at the group home when we came in '87. He had spent time at a juvenile lockup before coming here. He had shot and killed his stepfather, who was an alcoholic abuser who beat RB's mom and the kids. When he did well and was finished at the lock-up, he had come here. Mom, however, didn't change her ways or taste in men, and just found another abuser to be her boyfriend. When RB heard that this new guy was also beating his mom, he ran away to be with her and protect her. During the spring of RB's senior year at high school, when he was 18 and back living with his grandma, mom left the state with another, apparently similar, boyfriend.

RB was an excellent athlete, and was on the basketball and track teams, with an offer to play ball at the local junior college. He had the second fastest time recorded in the state that year in one of his track events, and if he did well at the regional track meet, he would be going to state to run against the boy with the fastest time. Just before the regional meet, mom called RB. Something had gone wrong, she said, and would he come up there right away, and also bring her some money. Leaving to help her again cost him the state track meet and his last semester of high school. Again, his loyalty to her and his impulsiveness had come at a cost to him. Let's all try to understand this: while your kids are young, it's your job to sacrifice for your kids. It's not their job to sacrifice for you. If all parents knew this, there would be very few kids in foster care.

KY, who had been with us for awhile, had just returned from a weekend with his mom. He had brought some more of his stuff here from home, and since lots of interesting things come here from home, we told him to place the stereo and suitcase up on the table by the front door to be checked. He willingly complied, but as he dropped the stereo onto the table, some cockroaches fell out and scurried around in every direction, looking for places to hide. As I was chasing these, he opened his suitcase, and more cockroaches were released for the hunt. I'm reminded of a truth they don't teach you in college: Don't get into this kind of work unless you are willing to teach kids how to blow their noses, help them to plunge out their toilets, shop for tampons, or chase and crunch cockroaches that are running around in your house. Have a sense of humor for the disgusting jobs, and pointed shoes to kill the cockroaches in the corners.

I had hoped that someday some of our kids could come back and work with us or even take our place. Some of the staff at New Horizons had been former residents, and it works well. Although some of our kids have offered, and many of them visit, none of them have worked here with us. One of our girls did become a foster parent. Sheria and Tamara have also been helpful here, at times, but they don't work with us.

One of our boys, Jon, may have come the closest to working here when he was working at the McDowell Center for Children, which is a group home/treatment center for boys with a higher level of needs, located here in Dyersburg. A couple of years ago, Jon went with me to Nashville, where we both spoke briefly to a large gathering of state legislators, group home and foster care agency administrators, and DCS staff. I was proud of Jon as he comfortably addressed a group that included the DCS Commissioner and the Lieutenant Governor of Tennessee, about his experience here and in foster care. I think he'll be a good dad to his son and a good husband to his wife, and I can't think of any more important accomplishment of which we would rather be a part. At least in this family, the cycle has been broken. This gives me hope that we can win this battle, one family at a time.

Chapter 17

MEDIC!

You can see the injuries. Now what can you do? Is there a treatment?

She died at 23, leaving a four-year-old son and a two-year-old daughter behind. Her step fathers had been abusive. She didn't know her biological dad very well. He didn't help plan or pay for the funeral. He couldn't help celebrate her life by getting up during her funeral and telling stories about her because he had none to tell. It's too late for him to make it up to her for the poor choices he had made that hurt her. It's too late for her biological mom to begin to protect her from abuse. If you are reading this chapter, however, then it's not too late for you to help our kids, our families, and our society. This book is one way in which I have tried to help the injured. I will suggest some ways in which you can help, too.

From the front line, I've given my report. I see an attack on our kids and our families, and I see the injured and what has caused the injury. Now I'm calling in the medics. A medic who is sent to an injured person is expected to stop and help ease the pain and begin to heal the injury. I hope this book has helped you to recognize the hurting kids around you. Now I will tell you how you can help with the healing. I have suggestions for those who are in, or could fulfill various roles in, the life of a hurting child or family.

Unwed dads:

Don't give up on your kids or your potential relationship and influence with your kids. If you are still reading by now, then I assume that you may hope to make up for your previous choices. I'm not against you; I'm for your kids. I offer you support and honesty. There will be pain, and there will be consequences in the lives of your kids, but don't give up hope for you or for them. Redemption is possible. It will require repentance, love, time, humility, money, maturity and self-sacrifice from you. Your kids and your relationship with them are worth all of this. Commit yourself to do whatever it takes to meet the needs of your kids and heal the hurt. I believe that if you do this, then you will be blessed.

Recognize the hurt you have caused, and honestly accept responsibility for your choices.

Be honest with your kids, and apologize to them for the unmet needs and poor example.

Don't have any more kids until you're married and can meet the standards in Chapter 12.

Can you marry your kids' mom? Would it be wise and would it work? Only you and she can answer these questions. Seek counseling or advice from someone mature. If you are currently living with her, then get married immediately. If you are no longer together, is there hope for reconciliation? I realize that there are situations and relationships that make marriage impossible or unwise, such as if you are married to someone else or have kids with other women.

If you can't marry, then cooperate with each other to meet all of the needs of the kids.

Pay your child support completely, willingly, and on time, even if it's a sacrifice. Your choices made you a parent, and your children's needs should come before your wants.

Follow the example of successful parents in Chapter Six. Spend time with your kids.

Commit to being enough of a man to wait to have sex again until you are married.

Unwed moms: (In addition to following the appropriate suggestions for unwed dads.)

Seek out and ask for help from mature men who can be father figures and role models.

Spend any child support money on meeting the needs of your kids, not your own needs. Any money that you get for your kids, including earned income credit, is to be used for the kids.

Get involved in a church which welcomes and serves the needs of unwed moms and fatherless kids. This will provide you with a support group for you and mentors for the kids.

Seek out a mentor for yourself. This could be your mom or someone in your church.

If you have little self-control, then use birth control.

Recognize that your taste in "men" has been poor. If he wanted sex before marriage or won't get married, then he is a boy and not a man. You can't have sex with a boy and then expect him to suddenly act like a man when you get pregnant. A boy will not do a man's job. Finding another guy just like him would make things worse. Have nothing to do with a guy who wants sex before marriage or is less than enthusiastic about sharing the responsibility for the kids you already have. If he already has kids by someone else, then ask yourself and him why he isn't with them and their mom. You probably need to "kick him to the curb." Some of the saddest relationships I have seen are between moms and the dads of whom the moms say, "It's worse with him here than with him gone! I can put up with the kids, but not him!" If you find yourself feeling this way or saying this about the guy you have chosen, then you have a hard choice to make. Make that choice only after considering the needs of your kids. It's not about your wants.

Legislators and government decision makers: Suggestions for you are in Chapter 14.

Your pro-family promises need to translate into action, results, and a good example.

If you are too intimidated by the anti-family bullies to protect kids, then you don't deserve to hold office. If you are influenced by anti-family money, then you are a sellout.

Children of unwed parents:

Without blaming your parents for your choices or the consequences of those choices, be honest to recognize the negative effect on your lives from the poor examples and choices by your parents. Forgive them. Don't imitate them. Don't excuse or justify their behavior.

Recognize that it's natural and common for kids to repeat the mistakes of parents, and to make similar choices in partners. Avoiding this will take honesty, maturity, wisdom, and strength.

Girls, if your dad is not around it will be very tempting to be attracted to older men. This attraction is not a sign of maturity on your part, but a result of your unmet need. If you are with a much older guy, then it is also probably a sign of immaturity on his part. Work with your family to find a man who can be a trustworthy, moral mentor to meet your need for a mature father figure, and he cannot be your sex partner. Your need is for a dad, not for a user. There are plenty of selfish, immature, perverted "men" who will want to take advantage of your unmet need in order to use your vulnerability to satisfy their desires. I don't want you to be hurt twice.

Boys, if your dad is not around, then you and your family need to understand your need and find a way to meet your need for a positive male mentor and example. Ideally, this need can be met by a member of your extended family, such as a grandfather or an uncle. Other ideas for mentors are your church youth leaders, Boy Scouts, teachers or coaches, or the father of a friend. Also remember that one sign of manhood is the ability to practice delayed gratification, and this is especially true in your sexual choices. Don't make another generation of fatherless children. Be enough of a man to wait until you are married to have sex, and for the mother of your children to never have to say about you that it's better for her and the kids without you than with you. I'm tired of hearing this condemnation of fathers from mothers. Stop the cycle of fatherless children with your generation, for your children.

Parents:

Meet the needs of your kids, so that they will not need to go to someone else to meet their needs for love and attention. Other chapters have suggestions for you, especially Chapter Six. The examples that you set are crucial! Listen and watch for opportunities to teach morals and character, and remember that sexual morals are critical to the health and future of your kids. Be extremely careful with entertainment choices.

Judges and juries:

Children and those who would hurt them must be made to understand that we are wise enough to place great value on children in our society. Any decision or judgment involving a child needs to reflect this value. These decisions include everything from child custody or placement cases to child abuse to protecting the unborn from murder. Send a clear message that abuse, neglect, rape, and older guys taking advantage of young girls will not be tolerated, and that our kids will be protected. Any judge who is not dedicated to protecting and providing for our kids is unfit to be a judge.

Remember as you make child placement decisions that an unmarried guy who is living with a mom, but is not the father of her kids, is the most common type of abuser in the home.

So far, there has been no "cure" for sexual predators, so keep them away from our kids.

Divorced parents:

It is crucial that you work together to meet the needs of the kids. For the sake of your kids, please pay careful attention to Chapters Six and Seven. The kids still need both of you. Don't let bitterness or selfishness blind you to your responsibility and to your kids' needs.

Churches, pastors, and church youth leaders:

Recognize that you are also on the front lines of a culture war. If you aren't in the fight for our kids and our families, then you aren't doing your job.

Teach the truth and confront lies. Don't be intimidated into silence by the PC bullies.

Identify and confront evil.

Along with the family, you are in the first line of defense against those who hurt our kids.

Welcome and serve unwed parents and fatherless kids. The church must be a safe haven where hurting families feel wanted and have the secure sense of belonging. Hate the sin but love the sinner. Provide male mentors for the fatherless kids in your church and community. Ask unwed moms and divorced moms how you can help. This help may include financial help or child care. Teach and expect the dads in your church to be men. Teach and expect everyone, especially the kids in your church, to reach out, welcome, and involve the fatherless kids in your community in the activities for the kids. Don't wait for the single parents or fatherless kids in your community to reach out to you. Reaching out is your responsibility. This may include some financial help for activities such as camps and trips. It also will include a willingness to love unconditionally. Set examples of how to be loving spouses and parents, how to confront evil, and how to forgive, welcome, and support those who repent of their previous poor choices.

Understand that hurting families need teaching that is relevant to the needs in their lives.

Follow the example of Jesus. In Chapter 8 of the Book of John, He demonstrates love, justice, honesty, grace, and mercy. He doesn't condone the sin or condemn the sinner to death. He didn't condemn her, but did identify the sin and said, "Go now and leave your life of sin." I assume that she was grateful to Him, and demonstrated her gratitude with repentance and obedience, because she called Him "Lord." He treated her with honesty, dignity, and love.

Put Jesus' teaching on judging others, in Matthew 7, to practice. This quote is often misquoted, misused, or twisted. It means that we are not to judge others unless we are willing to go by the same standards by which we judge others, and that we are not to be hypocritical. Be sure that, while you confront evil, you check for it in yourself, too. For an easy example, don't hire, ordain, coddle, or cover up for pedophiles in the church.

Fulfill the ancient mandates in Chapter 1 of James to meet the needs of orphans and in Chapter 1 of Isaiah to "Defend the cause of the fatherless."

Make sure your community has an alternative for unwed mothers, other than to murder the baby. Encourage your members and your community to adopt. Consider opening an adoption agency or crisis pregnancy center. Look for ways to support the adoptive and foster parents in your church or community. One idea is a free "mom's day out." Another is to provide all children's/youth activities free for foster children in your church, as our church has done for us.

Honestly evaluate whether or not you need to make some changes in order to meet the needs of fatherless kids or parents who need your support. I don't want to hear "We never did it that way before" from you!

Schools:

I already know that you recognize the special needs of fatherless kids. Teachers and administrators tell me that they can tell a fatherless kid by the difference in work, attitude, behavior, and success. You know that they need teachers and coaches to be mentors. You already understand that No Child Left Alone is even more important than No Child Left Behind.

Support parents by teaching the truth about the consequences of poor sexual choices. Teach and expect abstinence until marriage. Give truth and encouragement, not condoms.

Stay strong with a wise, modest dress code, and high standards of behavior, especially at your dances. Set a good example for your students.

If you are sexually attracted to students, then leave the teaching profession immediately. Have your needs met somewhere else. Seek professional help before you hurt a child.

Grandparents and other extended family members:

You have a critical relationship and responsibility with the kids in your family, especially to those without fathers. I am in your situation, myself, and am awed by the responsibility. Make sure the kids in your family are cherished, and sacrificially meet their needs. Meeting the needs of my granddaughter has slowed my progress on this book, but she is worth every moment.

Set a good, moral, consistent example. Don't make excuses for irresponsible sons.

Give your love and support to the unwed moms in your family, but honestly and lovingly show them how the choice to be an unwed mom hurts her, her kids, and everyone in the family.

Remember there is no substitute for time. Feeling sorry for the fatherless kids, spoiling them materially or excusing bad behavior is counterproductive. It's OK, however, to spoil them with lots of your time, love, affection, and attention.

Step parents:

You must already know that you have entered into a complicated relationship.

Your step kids will need to be assured that your spouse still loves them. Don't get into a competition with them for your spouse's love or time.

Don't put down your spouse's ex to or around the kids. Discuss differences away from the kids. Avoid a popularity contest for the kids with the ex.

Don't expect to take the place of the biological parent. It will cause resentment.

You can't call yourself a step parent just because you are living with or having sex with a child's parent. To be blunt, you are no kind of parent if you have chosen this lifestyle, and have no moral authority over the kids because of the immature example you set. Marry or move out!

For all of us:

We need to return to the kind of standards and society that values and cherishes our kids.

We need to recognize that there is a culture war and that our kids are the casualties.

We need to recognize that this war and the damage done to our kids will affect all of us.

We need to face the truth that abortion is a sign that our society does not recognize the value of our children. De-valuing kids is a sign of a society in decline, not of progress.

We need to model, practice, and teach the ability to delay personal gratification, and expect our kids to follow our example, especially in the area of sexual choices.

We need to understand that protecting kids trumps political correctness. Don't condone unwed parents. Instead, be aware of how much it hurts the kids for the parents to be unwed.

We need to understand that there are no "illegitimate" children, only illegitimate parents.

We all need to start right where we are, and work to make progress toward the ideal in each of our own families.

We need to use some old-fashioned peer pressure against unwed dads. Staying silent about what hurts kids also hurts kids. Spread the message that making and then abandoning babies is no longer acceptable. Irresponsible perverts need to feel some shame.

We need to accept the reality that we can't ignore the unwed dad problem and hope that it will go away or solve itself. Minimizing the problem will only let it continue. Pretending that kids aren't hurting will cause more pain. Remember, you didn't find this book in the fiction section.

We need to work to prevent another generation of fatherless kids, so our kids won't have to suffer and so our society won't have to try to fix the problems caused by disappearing dads.

We need to compel our current disappearing dads to be accountable for their actions.

We need to pay attention to what is happening to our kids, and realize that ignoring the needs of children, allowing the exploitation of children, or turning a deaf ear toward injustice to children comes at a steep price to our society.

"Politically correct" people:

I challenge you to honestly consider what I have observed, and to resist the temptation to deny reality when it doesn't further your agenda. If you really believe in tolerance, then you will be able to tolerate the suggestions I have made. If you really believe in diversity, then you will listen to a point of view that is not the same as yours, without trying to censor it or shout it down.

Recognize that you are part of the solution or part of the problem.

Call off your war against our kids and our families.

Stop condoning what is hurting our kids.   Get your values and priorities right.

If you "win" the culture war, you are dooming yourself, your kids, and your country.

Anti-family propaganda doesn't change the truth that a kid needs a mom <u>AND</u> a dad.

The truth and the needs of children are more important than your political agenda.

Your attempt to re-define family and marriage according to your agenda hurts children.

Your attempts to bully or intimidate those who are truly pro-family, and to deceive the public with name calling and truth twisting exposes you as the enemy of our children.

Entertainers, musicians, and those in the entertainment media:

Recognize your responsibility to our kids and our society. Enough with the excuses.

Face the damage you have done to our kids, and help heal it. Enough with the greed.

Honestly show our kids the damage from poor sexual choices. Enough with the lies.

News media:

Be honest! Don't replace the truth with your personal agenda.

Be fair in your reporting about those who are fighting to protect our kids and our families. For instance, it is dishonest and unfair to call pro-life activists, judges, or politicians "radical" while referring to pro-abortion activists, judges, or politicians as "moderate." It is dishonest and unfair, for example, to identify perverted priests as only a Catholic problem, when it is obviously also a homosexual problem. It is also dishonest to identify perverted politicians without also identifying the homosexual part of the perversion. To solve a problem, you must first correctly identify it, so don't be afraid to say that it is homosexual men who molest boys. It is unfair and biased to respond to those who are fighting for kids and families by referring to their views with words such as "repugnant." It is unfair to label family advocates as the "radical" Christian Right, while referring to anti-family forces as the "moderate" left. What is "moderate" about partial birth abortion or judges who give probation to child rapists? It is unfair and biased to be "sensitive" to all belief systems except Christianity. Ironically, when you do these things, you have actually exposed yourselves as the anti-family, anti-children "radicals."

How about featuring a "deadbeat dad" section of your newspaper or program? Show his name and a photo of him, along with a description of his neglected kids. Report how much money he makes and how much money he owes. Some photos of him spending his children's money at the casino or at a bar would make a great story! Warn readers or viewers against dating him.

How about an article or series exposing how weak dads weaken our country, or how all of us pay the consequences of irresponsible dads?

Take any celebrity who behaves, talks, dances, or dresses like a whore off of the news. Many of us are sick of seeing them and we don't want our little girls to imitate them.

Any individual who sees the hurt and wants to be a part of the healing:

Don't stay on the sidelines. Join the struggle to fight for kids in the culture war. The bad guys win when the good guys do nothing. Complacency in this battle hurts children.

Don't be intimidated by the anti-family bullies. Since these bullies include many in the media and many entertainers, they may make it appear as if those of us holding the moral high ground in the fight for children and families are outnumbered. However, if you stand up for the family, then you have the truth, nature, history, and the courage of your convictions on your side.

Look into being a foster or adoptive parent. If you can't adopt or be a foster parent, then see if there are agencies, clubs, organizations, or churches in your area that support such families, such as by raising money for Christmas gifts, through which you can help.

Each of us as individuals needs to recognize the value of kids. This includes our own kids and our society's kids. Our decisions need to be made with this value in mind. I know a guy who had a couple of kids by different girls. He didn't marry the mothers. He did list one of his children as a beneficiary of his life insurance, but didn't show that he valued his other child by also including her as a beneficiary, or paying child support. He didn't value either child or mother by marrying the mother, even though he claimed to "love" the mother and child. His death makes his second child and her mother face two additional tragedies: a child growing up without a dad and a mother trying to care for this child without the help of his life insurance benefits.

Volunteer to work with kids at your church or other local ministry or organization that works with kids. Look for the organizations and churches that work with fatherless or at-risk kids. These kids may need something as simple as a ride to an activity that normally would be provided by a parent, or something as complicated as a lifelong mentor.

Give money to organizations or churches that work with fatherless or at-risk kids. My favorites, of course, are the programs at the Mission Youth Center of the Dyersburg-Dyer County Union Mission. This is where I work here in Tennessee, but there are other good organizations that could use your help, too. I would encourage you to help local organizations and ministries.

Men, find a fatherless child to mentor. Your wife can mentor the mother and the child.

Show and teach your kids that a good marriage that lasts forever is possible and is a worthy goal. I thank my parents and Debbie's parents for the example they have set for us.

Teenagers, you can do your part to stop the cycle of fatherless kids in your generation. Don't have a baby until you are aware that you are not the center of the universe. (see Chapter12)

Voters, vote for legislators and judges who will value and protect our kids.

Don't make the problem worse. Make your sexual and marital decisions with the value of kids in mind. If you've already messed up and want to "fix it," then welcome to the fight! You now have the potential to be one of our greatest allies and make a great difference with kids. I wrote this book to help you and give you hope, not to condemn you.

Pray for our kids and for our families. Ask the designer of the family for guidance.

Don't spend your money on music or movies that glorify irresponsible sexual decisions. Give your support to entertainment that is clean and honest about the consequences of perversion.

Make mature choices based upon the truth that protecting and providing for your kids trumps personal gratification. Maybe we can avoid the need to use some of the ideas I presented in Chapter 14 by having wise priorities and by making wise decisions.

Don't be overwhelmed by the problems of unwed parents and fatherless children. We can protect our children one individual, one family, and one decision at a time.

His name was Bobby.   He and his brother had been abandoned by their father and later neglected and abused by their mother and her boyfriend. Bobby lived with us while his brother, who needed special care due to injuries resulting from the abuse, lived in a foster home. Both boys were well treated in the foster care system. Debbie and I, along with the other foster parents, case workers, and counselors were honored with an award from the Department of Human Services for our work with these boys. As everyone in the support system for these boys gathered for the ceremony with the governor in Nashville, a fact struck me as I counted how many people (and how much money!) that it was taking to try to meet the needs of these boys. All of our good work could not take the place of their parents. The sad reality was that even a dozen committed, loving, caring professionals, each doing their best, could never replace a pair of committed, loving parents. Human children weren't designed to have their needs met by professionals, but by parents! My goal and my challenge for each of you is to not allow stories such as this one to be the sad reality for any more kids.

Until every child has a family.